Why
PRAY ?

Bob Lively

TREATY OAK PUBLISHERS

PUBLISHER'S NOTE

This is a work of personal essay. All characters, events, and locations are based on the author's family and his experience. Any resemblance to other persons, living or dead, is purely coincidence and unintentional

ISBN-978-1-959127-00-0

Printed and published in
the United States of America

TREATY OAK PUBLISHERS
www.treatyoakpublishers.com

ACKNOWLEGDMENTS

This is my 15th book. And this will be my last book before I exit this world and enter into whatever goodness and mercy might await me. Just as I have done with my previous six books, I have elected to have this book published by Treaty Oak Publishers here in Austin, Texas. These folks are likely the best independent publishers in this state, if not the entire country. I've never been disappointed in their work.

And because I've chosen this publisher, I am privileged once more to have this work edited by Ms. Cynthia Stone. I can't imagine anyone possessing greater talent and a keener sense of nuance than Ms. Stone. She is a gift to any writer who longs to look better than he or she really is as a communicator.

In addition, I wish to thank Mr. Gregory T. Smith, who provided the cover art for this book. Greg is one of the finest artists in Texas, and it is a distinct privilege for me to have his art become the face of this small book.

Also, I wish to mention Ms. Kim Greyer, who in this part of the world is the "gold standard" for graphic artists. Ms. Greyer's students at Austin Community College are blessed to be taught by one of the very best in her field. Her design of this cover was yet another "masterpiece" of graphic art.

I also wish to thank my wife, Dr. Mary Lynn Rice-Lively, for her technical assistance every time I hit a roadblock or made a mistake. Only her patience exceeds her skill.

And as I mentioned in the introduction, I thank Ms. Ginny Booton for her suggestion that I write this book, and I thank my daughter Sarah for her consistent encouragement, and my 10-year-old grandson, Henry, for always being my partner.

DEDICATION

For my wonderful daughter,
Sarah Alice Lively Hill,

And for my equally wonderful grandson,
Henry Fontaine Hill,
both of whom are answers to prayer.

Introduction

Why do people pray?

I suspect this is a much better question for a group discussion than it is for the title for a book. That said: I also believe it's an important question to address because people have been praying to various deities ever since our paleo ancestors developed brains large enough to generate transcendent thoughts. And experience has convinced me that there are about as many reasons to pray as there are people who do pray.

The motives underlying humanity's penchant for prayer are connected to the dual axes of hope and angst, and these two axes are inextricably linked. As irony would have it, hope is in many respects the antidote to anxiety while, at the same time, it serves as the very driver of anxiety.

At the church I served in Dallas, a man once told me he had decided never again to hope for anything, and thereby, he would avoid the pain of disappointment. Of course, we are all free to choose this one path, but this way of thinking and—even more, of living—strikes me as a desperate attempt to hide from the inevitable vicissitudes of life. Life for every one of us is littered with disappointments and their attendant pain, but also with moments of great joy and soul-satisfying fulfillment.

Our ancestors hoped (and prayed) for the seasonal elements to vouchsafe them the bounteous harvest that would guarantee yet another year of survival. And, of course, underlying this hope always simmered the gnawing fear of famine and its devastating and, at times, lethal consequences.

In our world today, young students aspire to be admitted to the college of their choice while fearing the sting of rejection. New brides and new grooms, of course, hope the commitment they have made to each other will evolve into a life-long and happy marriage. And yet, if they are honest with themselves, they will admit their fear of becoming yet just one more divorce recorded in some county clerk's office.

Business people dream that their enterprise will prosper while they work, too often to the point of near exhaustion, to ward off the terrifying specter of bankruptcy and its accompanying stigma of failure.

So, it appears the duality of angst and hope are universal and invariably a part of the warp and the woof of human experience.

The one prodigious exception to this duality is revealed in the life of Jesus Christ. He came into this world to proclaim a whole new social structure he called both "the Kingdom of God" and the "Kingdom of Heaven." And throughout his brief three years of ministry he must have known that this proclamation would over time prove not only offensive, but also threatening. Rome not only viewed its empire as ordained by its panoply of gods, but also recognized its political ruler as a deity.

As a result, Jesus had plenty to worry about, and yet he went about his work free from the burden of fear, or even worry, for that matter. His life might best be summarized as a non-anxious presence that forever challenged the machinations of this world's anxiety-driven status quo.

St. Luke tells us in his Gospel that Jesus taught humanity to trust in God with such commitment and dedication as to give up the debilitating habit of anxiety. Jesus invites us to consider "the lilies of the field," as an analog to the universal and eternal truth that God will provide for us so as to render all our worries unnecessary.

But to be honest, most of us don't believe this to be true about our individual circumstances. We work and worry and allow the demon anxiety to drive us into a depression or into an early grave, or both.

I once counseled an elderly woman, who appeared at least to be the very portrait of piety. In her mind she did everything right: she never failed to attend worship in her suburban church, she tithed, she taught Sunday school to young children, she became a Stephen minister, and, of course, she prayed every day.

And yet, she came to see me in the hope that I might help her with what she described as her "terrible anxiety." I listened to her for a few sessions before I said to her, "What are you most worried about?"

Gasping at my question, she raised her head to reveal tears rolling down both cheeks. Her answer was as cutting as it was succinct. "Everything."

To ward off the very real possibility of us arriving at the same time to a dead end in this line of thought, I decided to pivot away from her obvious obsession with the absurd, not to mention grandiose, idea of viewing herself as the helpless and hapless "puppeteer" of the whole of human reality.

Her sudden display of exasperation did not dissuade her from tracking with me as I posed to her a far less threatening thought. "Tell me about your prayers," I said.

Of course, she told me that her prayers primarily centered upon asking God to make everything be good for herself and for all the people she cared about.

Once more I decided it was time to risk her interpretation of my next question as an attempt on my part to shame her. I hesitated while I considered just the right words. Following several moments of awkward of silence, I said, "How much do you actually trust God with your request for, at least, maintaining the status-quo of goodness in your life?"

She smiled and said, "Oh, I trust God completely, and why shouldn't I? Because my life is really very good."

I paused once more to allow her time to consider her all-too reflexive response to a question requiring a serious, and perhaps even courageous, probe into her own psyche and faith development.

And it was in those moments separating her pat answer and my silence that a small miracle occurred. Perhaps for the first time in her life, this woman discovered the uncomfortable truth she did not in fact trust the God to whom she had prayed for the whole of her life. She did not trust God to hear her daily prayers, much less to act on her behalf.

And in my experience, this woman's name is "Legion." While most of us claim to trust God with not only our lives, but also with the lives of those whom we love, we all too often fret, worry, and stress ourselves to the point of arresting our spiritual development with all kinds of unconscious ego tricks. But one of these tricks is to devolve into the kind of over-controlling and micro-managing person who goes through this life attempting to control everything and everyone in our sphere of influence.

But the One we claim as our Lord did not live this way. Read the four gospels with deeper attention and note that Jesus did not attempt to control others. No, he very clearly went about his three-year ministry inviting those he encountered to trust their Heavenly Father with everything about their lives. And the reason he could summon his listeners to consider the "lilies of the field" is because he trusted the One he called his Father with everything. Even on the very night he faced his own crucifixion, he appealed to his Father to take this cup (his agonizing death) from him, and yet, his next words expressed willingness for his Father's will to be done. And in this final petition, he demonstrated his readiness to trust his Father with even his horrendous execution at the hands of a Roman official, along with whatever might happen to himself and to his ministry following his death and burial.

Of course, it is both easy and tempting to say, "Well, after all, he was Jesus, but I'm merely an ordinary human being with flaws and at best, only a few minor neuroses."

But keep this in mind: centuries ago, the church established the truth that while Jesus was fully divine, he was also fully human. Yes, he was a man possessing the same capacity to experience fear as the rest of us, but again unlike most, he was willing to trust his Father to guide his every decision, even in those darkest final hours of his life.

I'm not alone when I declare that I'm convinced that such radical trust is far beyond my reach. Like most folks who try their best to follow Jesus, I all too often stress over any decision requiring even so much as the mere suggestion of courage. And before my retirement, I was no different than most adults inhabiting the 21st Century. I went into every new day convinced I would have to drive myself to succeed, no matter how I defined success at the time. I recognized I had to run hard until I ran on empty, and then I might pause only long enough to fill my tank up again, so once more I could run as fast as possible from the unimaginable consequences of failure.

An extraordinarily successful salesman once handed me a card containing two pen and ink drawings. One drawing was of a lion sleeping in a tall stand of savannah grass, and the other was of a gazelle standing in the same tall grass alert to the point of being hyper-vigilant. Printed on the bottom of the card was a sober declaration, followed by a searing question.

Every day in Africa a gazelle awakens to run for its life from a lion who awakens to the certainty that it too must run in the hope of catching and killing a gazelle so it can survive yet another day.

And the question was this:

So, which are you? A lion or a gazelle?

I smiled at the man as I held out his card, but in refusing to accept it, he frowned and said, "So which are you? Are you a lion or are you a gazelle?"

His overly-simplistic card spoke volumes regarding his worldview. From his perspective, he lived in a dog-eat-dog world where every day he had to rise even before the roosters and then venture out to outrun the competition before the competition could get the better of him. In my mind there could be little wonder why this successful businessman lived, or even survived, with a medical diagnosis case of colitis and hypertension, as well as an obvious general anxiety disorder. This man seemed to be a walking powder keg on the verge of suffering a suffering a stroke, a heart attack, or at best the onset of a major depressive episode.

Once more, he said in a sterner voice this time, "So, which are you, a gazelle or a lion?"

When I said, "Neither," he snatched the card from my hand and sighed his disgust. "So, then, tell me then what the hell are you?"

"I see myself as a child of God."

Frowning, the man said, "I don't think you can help me, sir." After which, he rose from his chair and made an abrupt exit from my office.

This man was so conditioned by his success as a salesman that he viewed his inhumane and unhealthy expectations for himself to be the price one must pay to be a responsible husband and father to three children. The idea of trusting One much higher than himself seemed just as much out of the question as any idea of slowing down and/or developing new disciplines of self-care. No, this man was certain that his self-punishing way of accumulating success was the only choice for how to live his life because, after all, this way seemed to work.

But, of course, the truth was that this man was killing himself and at some subterranean level of his consciousness, he must have known this to be true. And what struck me as so interesting about him was the irony of it all: He came to me seeking help, which he realized even before he called for an appointment, he would not be willing to accept. As a result, his visit was a waste of his time and mine.

Nevertheless, this brief interaction with this man reinforced in my mind the crucial role prayer plays in our lives. I believed this to be of utmost importance in the moment this exhausted man made his hasty exit. However, I was at the same time certain I could never convince this man of anything, no matter how long he gave me to try.

No, convincing doesn't ever work for the simple reason that all truth must be discovered. In fact, if someone does not discover it for himself or for herself, it remains forever, at best, a mere possibility, or worse, one more useless opinion. But allow a person the opportunity to first discover, and then to embrace, a new reality as truth, and that individual will make that truth their own.

I never did hear from the man again, so, of course, I have no idea if he ever gave up the idea of living as though he was either a gazelle or a lion. But in retrospect, I'm glad he showed me the card with the text he accepted as his core truth, because it played a part in compelling me to write this book, my last one before, as in the words of the bard, "I shuffle off of this mortal coil."

But to be clear, I didn't write it to convince anyone

of anything. No, I wrote it in the hope of affirming those who pray, and as an invitation of sorts to those who see no real value in prayer to discover the truth and the power of prayer on their own. After more than four decades in the pastoral ministry under the Presbyterian banner, I have come to believe through the experience of discovery that prayer is the gateway to all true mental health and to all real spiritual growth.

And my sincere hope for this small book is that it will serve the Kingdom of God as a useful instrument in bringing you, the reader, into a closer and more meaningful relationship with God.

Chapter 1

What is prayer?

T his question is likely *the* most profound interrogative any human being can pose, regardless of his or her faith tradition and/or station in life. So, what is prayer? The most honest answer I know to offer is to suggest that prayer is a mystery. And this is so because prayer first introduces us and then connects us to the Ultimate Mystery of all perceived reality.

While one might come to "know" God through the discipline of earnest prayer, no human mind can ever fully comprehend the One to whom we pray, because God remains forever incomprehensible. As a result, God requires us to surrender our capacity for reason for the much greater gift of faith. We are to accept Absolute Mystery as the Lord of our lives while journeying through the years we are given to live.

This is a daunting challenge, but it appears far less difficult, for those who have been blessed with sufficient faith to pray with discipline.

But again, trusting our lives and the lives of those we love to a Mystery, and demonstrating that trust with the willingness to pray is never an easy decision. By our natures, we have come to rely upon our ability to reason as *the* most reliable way to perceive reality and, thereby, discover solutions to our problems. From the very beginning, we've been conditioned to apply reason as our foremost guide through life. A willingness to pray requires the famous Kierkegaardian "leap of faith."

I spent one-third of my life in some kind of classroom where I first learned to read Dick and Jane stories when I was only five to a time twenty years later when I was taught first to read and then to exegete ancient Hebrew texts. And through every learning experience and with each new challenge, I relied solely upon my reason to succeed as a student. For the most part, reason served me well as I matriculated on schedule from one instructional level to the next.

But, it is only by faith in Something, or more accurately in *Someone*, far greater than myself, that I later learned to place my trust. And it is to that same Someone that I pray. When I was a child, I learned to call that Someone "God," but years later I discovered that Jesus called the same Someone to whom he prayed, Abba, or if you will, "Daddy."

Over the centuries many people have entered into a similar intimacy, with the result that they came to regard this Mystery as a loving and caring Father who is directly and deeply involved in their lives.

Although we speak of God as our "Heavenly Father" each time we utter the words of "The Lord's Prayer," many folks still find it difficult to think of the Ultimate Mystery of all human experience as being a loving and caring Father. They cannot see God as bidding us to place our trust in this One we cannot even begin to comprehend.

One of the favorite positions I held over a forty-plus-year career in the pastoral ministry was to serve as a chaplain in a drug and alcohol treatment center. This experience allowed me to appreciate the genius of the 12 Steps to recovery. I was so impressed with the efficacy of this program of healing that I even wrote a book viewing each of the steps through the prism of reformed theology.

The real genius in the 12 Step program is that it invites each participant to discover this truth: only the non-doctrinal God of their own subjective appropriation can restore them to sanity. The implications are as gripping as they arc important. Among them are these five:

Every individual is free to choose to think about God in whatever way makes the most sense to him or to her.

Each participant is invited to discover that the disease of addiction has caused them to become insane.

Every recovering person is granted the time and the space necessary to discover that God, *and God alone*, can restore them to sanity. And it is through this discovery that the recovering person experiences the transformation from an ego-defended and ego-driven existence to a whole new way of thinking and living which is grounded in God's will.

Every recovering person is free to surrender all negative drivers in their life, such as fear, resentment, and rage, to God in exchange for a radical new way of being a human being, or what St. Paul referred to as, "becoming a new creation in Christ."

And last, but most important, every recovering person discovers that prayer is essential to their recovery, because it is prayer that connects them to God and keeps them in touch with God's will for their lives. Hence, in addition to being a mystery, prayer is also a connection to God.

And what I find most intriguing about this connection is that through it all, God remains incomprehensible, yet by the means of prayer, God can also become known. In no way does this imply that the one who prays can comprehend the Mystery of God. Rather it means that through the discipline of earnest prayer, one can, and often does, come to know God, much in the same way any person comes to know a trusted friend or mentor. And this kind of knowing might best be described as a personal relationship.

Any human being who feels so moved can enter into a relationship with the incomprehensible Mystery, Who is God. Once more, we don't have to comprehend God to enter into an intimate relationship with the very Creator of the Universe. All that is required for the establishment of a meaningful, even transformative, relationship with God is one's willingness to pray.

I don't remember when I first prayed, but it was probably when I was a four or five year old student in a wonderful Presbyterian kindergarten where our teacher, Mrs. Louise Neeley, taught us to recite the words of "The Lord's Prayer." At the time, I no more understood those words than I did all the other big words I heard adults using, but I've always been grateful that this good woman taught me so early in my life this truth: prayer is of utmost importance.

I began the second grade in a small private, church-sponsored school, but by the end of my second week in that school my parents decided to transfer me into the large public elementary school close to our house.

I felt a bit overwhelmed on my first day in that big school for several reasons. First, I was a year younger than my classmates due to the fact that I had been enrolled in a private school during my year in first grade. And second, I was a bit taken aback by the sheer size of the class. My previous class consisted of no more than ten children, but this class registered twenty-five or so second graders, all of whom were well acquainted with each other.

And last, I felt embarrassed right away that I had chosen to wear the same pair of old scuffed shoes that I had worn to my previous school. In retrospect, I wonder how my ever-vigilant mother allowed me out of the house in those old shoes, but somehow I managed to slip past her careful and discerning eye that morning.

And much to my humiliation, one of my new class-mates not only noticed my shoes but called the entire class' attention to the sad state of my foot wear. His voice rung out across that classroom with the clarity of a fire drill bell. "Hey, look at the new boy's shoes."

This boy's summons was punctuated by the entire class-room laughing at me. And in that terrible and memorable moment, I wanted to die, but fortunately, a compassionate and seasoned teacher intervened with questions posed to the class as a way of distracting the class from noticing the tears fast filling my eyes as a prelude to the sobs that followed.

But it was in that wonderful, yet terrible day, that I made a significant discovery in the form of a girl named

Suzanne. She was, without question, the prettiest little girl I'd seen in my entire five years of living, and as best I could tell, she was not only the teacher's favorite but the class' favorite as well.

What impressed me most was the fact she was the only student in that class who knew how to spell the word, "people." And what none of us could have known then is that this pretty little girl would one day be our senior class valedictorian out of a class of five hundred students.

So, right then and there on my first day in public school, I decided I wanted a girlfriend. Of course, I had no idea what it meant to have a girlfriend other than the fact that some of my buddies in the first grade had claimed to have girlfriends.

Therefore, in the presence of one so pretty and so smart, I determined that if I was ever going to have a girlfriend, Suzanne would be the one. No other little girl even came close to her beauty and obvious talent.

That very night following my first day in public school, I climbed into bed and closed my eyes to pray a primitive and, of course childish prayer. I whispered, "Dear God, please make Suzanne like me. Amen." I had not yet even learned her last name, but I figured God knew it."

Following my prayer, I lay in my bed for a while, pondering my chances. I was quick to admit that I was not all that attractive. In the first grade, I never did advance beyond the second reading group, I had no idea how to spell "people," and I usually struck out when I swung a bat.

The more I contemplated my chances, the more I realized that I was not all that great a catch.

Nevertheless, I walked into that big school the very next morning spurred on by an unfamiliar, but still euphoric hope filling my heart.

And before I managed even to offer a friendly smile to the little girl who had won my heart, another little girl ran in my direction to inform me in a whisper that none other than Suzanne had told her she liked me. I'm sure my eyes bugged out, or at least I must have gasped.

And that was all it took for me to realize that I had figured out how this prayer business worked. In fact, the more I thought about it, the more I realized that God was even more efficient than Santa Claus. With God, gratification was almost immediate, while Santa always involved a protracted waiting period where I would have to eat my vegetables and refrain from hitting my little brothers.

For me, at age five, God was a mere celestial Santa Claus. All that was required of me was to close my eyes, then ask. And in a matter of hours, it (whatever the object of my longing happened to be at the time) would be mine.

My friendship with Suzanne never did blossom into a romance. And fortunately through good instruction from the teachers in my Presbyterian Church, my views on prayer evolved over time to the point where I learned the importance of praying for others while praying for myself with all sincerity that God would continue to make me "a new creation."

One of the most disturbing discoveries in my four-plus decades of ministry was how many otherwise accomplished adults prayed as though the Almighty was some kind of celestial slot machine whereby they might achieve for themselves all manner of good fortune and things if only they couched their requests employing just the right words before pulling the lever with a final, "Amen."

I've spent years listening to folks who told me their prayers were little more than begging God for what they believed they wanted and/or needed.

And it is precisely this kind of spiritual immaturity that has given rise to what we today know as the so-called "Prosperity Gospel. "The "Prosperity Gospel" is a theological scam and a grotesque perversion of the very Gospel Jesus preached. The scam works this way: Some televangelist convinces the gullible that all they need do to rise out of the harshness of poverty is to "plant a seed," in the form of a financial gift to the televangelist.

The theological principle promised here is that the so-called seed gift will be blessed by the Almighty and will then be returned several fold to the donor. The formula is as simple as it is cruel: Give to God in care of this televised grifter and receive in return up to ten times, or even more in return.

Without fail, the televangelist becomes fabulously wealthy on the backs of the spiritually immature, and only God knows how much damage this crime has done to well-meaning, but gullible, folks who were led to believe that God is nothing more than a heavenly ATM.

In my view, it's healthy to ask God for what we believe we need, such as good health for ourselves and for those whom we love. But making of our prayers nothing more than a long string of requests is to misunderstand the core purpose of prayer, and even more, to keep ourselves stuck in an immature view of who God is and what God is about.

So then, what is the purpose of prayer if it is not to ask, or even beg, Heaven for what we believe we need or want? Over the more than seven decades I've been given to live, I've come to believe that prayer does, indeed, have an end or, if you will, a purpose, or what the ancient Greeks called a *telos*.

And today I see that the purpose of prayer is to keep the one who prays in a close connection to God, with the result being that the one who maintains that connection might evolve into a holy man or woman.

And this evolution, or transformation, occurs far more often than we might imagine, with perhaps the most obvious example being the Apostle Paul. He began his life as a brilliant religious zealot, even to the point of becoming a sociopath. Over time and by the power of being connected to God by prayer, he was transformed into a holy man who changed the course of Western history by bringing the Gospel of Jesus first to ancient Greece.

Far less dramatic transformations occur all the time. I've been acquainted with many men and women who have evolved into holy people following years of prayer in the course of working the 12 Steps of recovery. I've also known folks who were in no way involved in recovery who have evolved into holy people.

So now, the question becomes this: What is a holy person? Borrowing from the words of the Apostle Paul, I view a holy person as one who "lives by the Spirit." Furthermore, these people inherit the gifts of the Spirit, which are "love, joy, peace, patience, kindness, generosity fruitfulness, gentleness, and self-control." *(Galatians5:22-23)*

Each time you encounter a person possessing these gifts, you have most likely encountered a holy person, and you have discovered a life that has long been connected to God through the discipline of mature prayer.

The writers of Genesis tell us we are made in the very image of God, and those who have become holy have evolved into what some recognize as the true self. The false self is the one we create, which is driven and guided by the ego, or what I like to call the 'homemade' self. In St. Paul's language, the false self lives by the flesh, while the true self lives only by the Spirit.

Those who live in the true self are the most fortunate people on Earth because they have discovered the truth that this life is in the end only about one thing: expressing love. The gifts of the Spirit are theirs for the asking, and since they live by the Spirit, their lives are marked by joy.

However, those who live only by the flesh exist in the image they, themselves, have created. And for the whole of their lives, they live the error that this life is primarily about them in general, and in particular about their being successful, impressive, and even celebrated. To their misfortune, their lives are driven by anxiety and marked by regret and disappointment.

Just imagine how their distorted lives would change if they took all that worldly wealth and specious attention and lavished it on the ones Jesus instructed us to care for: the hungry, the sick, the suffering, the widows and orphans, the least of us. If they could give up the notion that they have to come first, and by their actions show love instead, they would find true joy. If they realized they were created in God's image, not the other way around, they might find their way to live by the Spirit.

Chapter 2

"The Power and the Glory"

everal years ago, I was invited to gaze at the heavens through the most powerful telescope operated by the University of Texas' McDonald observatory located on Mt. Locke in far west Texas. I was more than a little thrilled to receive this opportunity, and as I peered into this magnificent telescope, I spied but two forms. Barely visible were two comma-shaped objects that remained clear, but still strangely faint.

After studying these distant formations for only a few seconds, I turned to the astronomer who assisted me and said, "What are those things?"

He said, "They are nebulae."

"But what are they?"

"Each one is composed of billions of galaxies," was his matter-of-fact response.

Now intrigued, I said, "How far away are they?"

"Oh, about 200 million light years away."

"And what's beyond them," I said.

"God," was his one-word answer, which he offered with a smile.

That night as I lay in bed, I pondered the amazing discovery I had made that cold night on Mt. Locke. How could the Creator of a universe so vast, so majestic, and still so unexplored, be at all interested in the life of one such as me, who is only extraordinary in his abject ordinariness? I couldn't even begin to ponder such a question, so I lay still until sleep arrived to ease the pain that attends attempting to comprehend the wholly incomprehensible. Days later I reflected on the prayer Jesus taught to his disciples, and in particular his descriptors, until "glory" and "power" arrived to comfort me in my futile struggle.

Could it be that the Author of this infinite and ever-expanding universe not only knows us as individuals, but is also invested in our welfare and actively involved in even the mundane matters of our personal lives? Could it be possible that we are, as Scripture claims, created in the very image of this incomprehensible God? And finally, could it be that each one of us is far more than a mere mass of protoplasm, or an accident in the evolutionary process of natural selection?

The whole of Scripture in general, and Jesus specifically, teaches us that the very Creator of all that exists is our Heavenly Father. And furthermore, this God is a caring, loving, and forgiving Father, who so loves all who inhabit this world that he gave us His only Son.

And He gave us his beloved Son so that we might come to view him as One who is not only knowable, but intimately involved in each one of our lives.

When I juxtapose the God of Scripture against the backdrop of what I saw in the telescope that dark night on the summit of Mt. Locke, many words come to mind, but one seems most appropriate. And that word is "glory," as it is meant in the conclusion of this timeless prayer when we say, "for thine is the Glory…"

The universe reflects the glory of its Creator just as God's willing intimacy with us reflects the amazing glory of his grace.

Each time I reflect on my very imperfect life, I discern one grace-filled event after another. And when I turn serious regarding this reflection, I can see that from the very beginning, God's grace has guided me every step of the way, even in the wake of my mistakes and even when I was foolish enough to wander far off the path that was and is today God's will for my life.

During my first week of college at a small, Presbyterian liberal arts college in North Texas, I was required to fill out a form stating my vocational goals. Feeling more than just a little self-conscious, I checked the box marked ministry. Of course, at the time I didn't believe I was good enough or even smart enough to pursue such a career. I recognized what I regarded to be the truth about myself: I was a kid of no more than average intelligence, a frequent mistake-maker, and even somewhat of a fraud, since I had somehow managed to convince the folks back home in my high school and in my church that I was a young man with a something to offer.

By the time I reached my senior year in college, I had solidified my plans: I would become a teacher in a public school in some midsized Colorado town where I would be active in the local Presbyterian Church, and perhaps even assist with the coaching of a Little League team, or some such program. I would marry my girlfriend, who at the time was a student at the University of Texas, and together we would live out our lives in the high country while making positive contributions to the life of some community. I did my student teaching in a local junior high school that final semester in college. And I earned such good reviews that the school's principal even offered me a job for the following year.

As far as I could tell, my life appeared good and my future bright, all except for one terrible, mitigating obstacle: the Vietnam War. The college taught me critical thinking, and the more I read about this war and thought about it, the more I came to believe that this whole bloody conflagration was illegal and immoral. Further, this "conflict" was predicated upon the ridiculous lie that if we did not stop the communists in Saigon, San Francisco would be the next to fall.

I was on the very cusp of graduating with my degree in one hand and a teaching certificate in the other, when the so-called Tet Offensive occurred, causing President Lyndon B. Johnson, a fellow Texan, to double down on the war effort by drafting more and more young men, such as myself, who were newly-minted college graduates. The recruiters who visited our campus tried to convince me that I would serve as an officer due to my newly-acquired education. But what they didn't bother to mention was the well-published truth that in this guerrilla war, first and second lieutenants were the first to be shot.

In the spring and summer of 1968, I knew I didn't want to die at age 21, but I couldn't figure out what to do to escape being thrust into a war I could in no way support. I couldn't see any possible way out of it. I was not, in truth, a conscientious objector in the purest sense of that position. And once more I considered seminary, but I knew it would not be right to go to the seminary for all the wrong reasons. So I gave up on the idea of becoming a minister simply because one had to be called to do such work, and yet I had no idea whatsoever what that meant. So for the whole of my final semester in college, I languished in a constant state of depression and dread.

First, and foremost, of course, I wanted to live. And I also wanted to teach to teach kids how to write and how to appreciate literature and our history. I planned to get married to the beautiful and brilliant young woman I loved, and I looked forward to becoming a father some day and to pursuing a graduate degree in American studies. But the sum of my dreams seemed to evaporate before my very eyes each time I reminded myself that the government meant to send me into harm's way to fight in the most unjustified war in American history up to that time.

Most every evening that spring semester, I ventured to the college student union where I sat alone in a booth and pondered my bleak options before I decided to pray. My prayer was simple and anything but heroic. All I knew to pray were these three words: "Help me. Amen."

One night in April of that year, I received somewhat of a mild revelation. It dawned on me that our government was fighting two wars at the same time. One war was being waged against a proud peasant people in Vietnam, while the other was a battle against poverty under the aegis of President Lyndon Johnson's "Great Society" program.

While I was certain that one war was an abomination, I decided the other war was noble and right, and even more, likely blessed by God. And on that very night I discovered a notice on a college bulletin board announcing what was called "The Teacher Corps." I mailed in my application the following morning. After a long anxious summer of waiting, I received word of my acceptance, and therefore for the time being was deferred from the draft.

In September of that year, I enrolled as a graduate student in the predominantly Black university which hosted the Teacher Corps. In December I was married to my longtime girlfriend, who was completing her under-graduate degree at the University of Texas.

By the first of the year, I was assigned to teach in a tiny rural school district fifty miles east of Austin. For the most part, I taught the Black children of migrant workers how to read. But my favorite class consisted of reading to the small group of kindergarten children. One unforget-table morning, I noticed a little girl slumped forward in her chair with her head in her hands.

Once the story was done, I approached her and touched her forehead to discover she was burning up with fever.

Right away, I picked her up and carried her to the school nurse, who was quick to inform me that this child, whose name was Letha, needed to be sent straight home. I nodded before inquiring how we could send her home when her family likely owned no telephone and, needless to say, no car or truck. The nurse drew me a crude map of where she thought Letha lived.

So with Letha in my arms, now wrapped in a borrowed wool blanket, and with a map stuck in my shirt pocket, I struck out for the general vicinity of Letha's family's home. After several dead ends and detours, all of them on dirt roads, I happened upon a primitive cabin with smoke pouring out of a stone chimney. A braying donkey was tied to a big loblolly pine adjacent to small sagging porch. For the first time little Letha sat up and pointed through my dusty windshield. "Here."

I parked the car and walked around to the passenger side to retrieve the tiny girl. And with this precious little four-year-old secure in my arms, I approached a front door so battered by the elements that it hung crooked on a pair of rusty hinges. Knocking proved unnecessary, as an elderly woman stepped onto what few floor slats remained on the rickety porch to take the child from me. Letha wrapped her arms about the old lady's neck. I don't think I even introduced myself as I stepped into a cabin resting on a dirt floor.

I did, however, linger long enough to tell the woman the obvious: little Letha was sick and needed to come home.

Still holding her granddaughter tight, the woman said, "You from the school?"

"Yes, ma'am." And with that, I made my exit and stepped far beyond the range of that surly donkey's hind legs and returned to school.

Only later did I find out what I expected. Letha was

only four and had been allowed into the kindergarten class so that she could be assured of two meals every day.

I now believe my brief experience with little Letha sealed my call into the ministry. For on the way back to the school, I pondered the injustice of people forced by all manner of complex circumstances to subsist in such abject poverty. While I agreed with the lofty and noble goals of the administration's Great Society, I decided in that moment that any real change that might bring about a more just world would most likely be a grassroots effort on the part of people of faith far more than it ever would the product of some government program, no matter how well conceived and funded. As a result, I reconsidered the idea of enrolling in a seminary.

Four and one-half years later I was ordained into the old Southern Presbyterian Church, which is now the Presbyterian Church in the USA. And following a brief pastorate as a campus minister and instructor in religion at a tiny college in Arkansas, I landed on the pastoral staff of a large Presbyterian church in downtown Dallas.

Again, in retrospect, one of my greatest disappointments in the ministry was to discover just how indifferent to the plight of the poor and the marginalized the people of faith I served were. For the majority, church was safe and cool in summer and warm in winter, a place to come hear all about Jesus from a gifted orator, and then sing sweet hymns, all in the name of calling themselves Christians.

It required only a month or two for me to become certain that I'd made a huge mistake by signing on with this church. The more I read theology, the more I became convinced that Paul was right when he claimed that the church was the living body of Christ in this world; and the longer I served in that particular church, the more I came to realize that the lay leadership of this body did not appreciate either my views, or me.

I was giving serious thought to moving on when in the fall of that first year an older, wiser, and much more experienced pastor announced his intention to open a soup kitchen to feed the dozens of homeless folks who came through our doors each day searching for a bite of their daily bread. This older colleague invited me to join him in this endeavor, and for the next ten years I directed this program which, at the time of this writing, has served more than eight million meals to the desperate of Dallas.

In those ten years, I was privileged to serve a church that never embraced me. Yet that congregation assisted in the founding of an all-night shelter for the homeless, a freestanding battered women's shelter, the founding of a free housing ministry for homeless families, a jail ministry, summer day camp for the children in the poorest of Dallas' neighborhoods, a Bible school every Saturday for those same children, and a summer youth program where high school kids from all over the state came to work in the soup kitchen and serve as leaders in the day camp.

It was a remarkable decade in the life of that old downtown church and in my life as well, and it all occurred because of God's truly amazing grace. Believe me, it's not at all easy to serve a congregation that rejects you, but it can be done. I know this to be true because I did it, and I still bear the scars, psychological and otherwise. But let me be clear, it can only be done because God is love and because grace both guides and protects one who is as naïve and as limited intellectually as I happen to be.

Grace abounds and is always available, but it is most accurately perceived in the context of prayer. For me, prayer became in those difficult years the sustaining power of my very existence. Every time I recite the words of Jesus, "For Thine is the Power", I know in my heart what it means to be sustained by that very Power.

And even though that decade was the most difficult of my life, it did teach me two very important lessons:

1. To trust wholly in God's grace, and
2. To pray.

Chapter 3

The power of prayer

O ver the four decades of my ministry, I've lost count of the many times people said when faced with some hopeless situation, "I guess now all we can do is pray."

And in saying this, what they in fact meant is that all too often we have relegated prayer to the rank of one last desperate measure. But the truth is that prayer should be the first thing we do, and the unceasing thing, and also the final thing.

Because once more, prayer is what connects us to God. And because all things are possible with God, by nature it follows that prayer is powerful.

Now here's a question many have posed to me over the years:

Does prayer change the course of our lives?

My answer is always a resounding "Yes!" Although I'm quick to say I have no idea how prayer works, I do not believe it is a matter of us employing precisely the right words or complying rigidly with any one tradition or ritual.

That said: I have experienced the power of prayer

working in my life for the whole of my life. My dear mother was raised in a devout Christian home in a small town in North Texas where daily prayers were a big part in the warp and woof of her family. And, I know for a fact that all her life she prayed for me and my three brothers.

There were some terrible times in my college years when I felt very isolated and lonely. In those dark moments, I would think of her and could almost hear her prayers of intercession for me.

During a heartwrenching time in my ministry in Dallas, I risked my career to convince the church to purchase a derelict six-plex apartment building for the purpose of providing free temporary housing to homeless families. The church leadership made it clear, in fact, abundantly clear, that it was up to me alone to raise the necessary funds to renovate this old building.

Every estimate I received from various contractors topped one-quarter of a million dollars. Of course, I recognized my neck was on the proverbial chopping block if I didn't raise this money. Desperate men, women, and children would get no second chance for housing, and I would most likely be invited to terminate my always uneasy relationship with this venerable old church.

Nobody I knew from anywhere else had indicated any genuine interest in providing housing for homeless families. So, the way I saw it, it was up to us or it was not to be.

I wrote grants and mailed letters to any group I hoped might help us. Feeling more than a little worried, one cold February morning, I drove to this derelict complex, which was located in what the Dallas Police Department called "the War Zone." This neighborhood was generally regarded as the most dangerous in all of Dallas.

After parking in front, I turned the key and let myself into one of the empty downstairs apartments where I settled on the floor because, of course, there was no furniture. I'd like to report that I entered into some kind of prayer, but if I did, I don't remember.

All I do recall is spying a battered old trunk resting in one corner of the room. Curiosity got the better of me, and I crawled across that room on all fours.

As I raised its heavy lid, a cloud of dust brought on a loud sneeze. My eyes widened when I discovered the thing was filled with all kinds of papers, including paper money in various denominations. Curled up next to the old trunk, I sorted through the variety of papers that had long been stored inside. It didn't take me more than a few minutes to discover I had purchased a building that had once been a notorious house of ill repute known throughout all of South Dallas as "Sadie's".

As I sat alone on that cold floor, I could only chuckle at the thought of the oh-so-respectable and conservative congregation I served now being the owner of an old "bawdy house." In an instant, I made the necessary iron-clad decision not to tell anyone, other than a couple of trusted colleagues, the exact history of our newly-purchased property.

Later I did report the box to a dependable financial officer, who retrieved it from the property and pulled from its dusty confines more than twenty thousand dollars in small bills. All of that money was reinvested in the renovation of the building.

A few minutes before I abandoned the property that day, I happened to pull open a kitchen drawer where I discovered a small scrap of paper bearing the following three words written in pencil: "Prayer changes things."

And in that poignant moment, I decided to give up worrying about attracting the necessary funds to this old house, and I permitted myself to embrace the truth: this very risky, new venture had never been mine, but had all along belonged wholly to God.

By trusting the Almighty to see this thing through, I relaxed, and soon sufficient grant money arrived to complete the renovation. Each adult Sunday School class "adopted" an apartment and, after decorating the walls with framed landscapes, filled it with the necessary furniture.

Less than a year after my discovery of the scrap of paper in that drawer, we welcomed into our newly renovated apartments our first tenant, a lovely, young Black single mom with a five-year-old daughter named "Precious." After the prescribed ninety days, Precious and her mother moved into their own apartment, which was near the pharmacy where the mom had secured a job as a cashier.

Dozens of tenants came and went, with each family being far more stabilized when they left than when they first came to us seeking shelter.

A few months after a small group of the church leadership masterfully arranged for me to make a peaceful and dignified exit from the church, the six apartments were donated to a new entity known as The Dallas Interfaith Housing Coalition.

As far as I know, that expanded ministry continues today, and for that I am most thankful.

Several years ago, I was invited to preach at a church in Austin, Texas, my new home town. And in the context of that sermon, I told the story of the founding of our housing ministry. I concluded that proclamation with these words: "Throughout the course of my life, I never ever saw any prayer turn a sow's ear into a silk purse, but I did once upon a time witness prayer turn a whorehouse into a safe haven for desperate families."

While still in college, I enjoyed another memorable experience with prayer. I will preface this anecdote with the personal awareness that in all likelihood I have a learning disorder when it comes to math. It's not that I'm no good at it, it's just that I can't see it. In all three years of high school, I made straight As in my other subjects, but struggled in math.

Several adults in my church collaborated to convince me to apply to an excellent small liberal arts college located only 75 miles from my hometown.

For the first three years of college, I avoided any course having to do with math. However, by my senior year, further avoidance proved impossible. In the last week of my junior year, I signed up to take a physics course for non-science majors in the coming fall semester. I knew I would struggle, but I had no real choice in the matter. Either take and pass "baby physics," as the course was known, or not graduate.

For the whole of that summer, I carried my worry with me when once more I worked on a ranch in Colorado. I'm certain my angst was so heavy that my horse could feel the extra weight each time I pulled myself into the saddle.

After weeks of dread and worry, I found nothing to help alleviate the excruciating pain that attends the thought of failing at something as important as one's future. So I decided to pray. And in no way did I intend my prayer to be a substitute for the work that would be required.

One beautiful summer morning on a rare day off, I discovered a room in one of the many small visitor centers in Rocky Mountain Nation Park. I sat alone in that cozy room for perhaps a half hour, studying the magnificent scenery. At last, I bowed my head and whispered these memorable words, "Father, I need your help like never before. Amen."

That fall when I returned to campus, I attended my first "baby physics" class where I discovered a kindly old professor, who had been called out of retirement to teach a course I suspect no other professor wanted to have anything to do with. By the end of that semester, I managed to maintain an unspectacular, but still passing, grade in that course.

But the grade on my final exam would still determine the question of my graduation. Two weeks before the scheduled exam, the professor handed out a paper containing 100 problems. He next informed us that 10 problems from this work sheet would be on the final.

I carried that paper to my dormitory room and did my best to work the problems, only to realize within moments that my efforts were in vain. I couldn't make heads or tails of the problems on that page, now taunting me like one hundred cruel tormentors. For an hour or so, I sat at my study desk, staring at the one hundred mysteries that were either the gateway to a bright future or the last pitiful whimper of my academic career.

As those vexing puzzles generated a swirling fog in my mind, a knock came at my dorm room door. I answered it to find a young man standing before me with an obvious case of worry twisting his face toward misery. I called him by name, then said, "What's going on?"

"Man, I need your help. We have our poem explications due next week in old Dr. ____'s class, and I can't figure out anything T. S. Eliot is saying in these poems. After all, I'm a physics major, so why do I need to know anything about what some poet writes? This time next year, I hope to be flying jets over in 'Nam.

I grinned so hard my face ached. "Perhaps we can work something out."

With that, I turned to my desk and handed him my work sheet. He scanned it for no more than a few seconds. "You've got to be kidding me, Lively. A third-grader could work these things."

"But I can't," I said, and in that moment we made a deal: I would unlock the mysteries of the T. S. Eliot poems that had him stumped, and he would open my mind to problems intended for a third grader.

Of course, neither of us did the other's work. My friend taught me a new (to me) way of thinking about the problems, and, in time, I caught on well enough to solve all 100 problems just a day or so prior to the final. I did much the same thing for him by choosing a non-assigned Eliot poem and explicated it. I offered it to him as a template, which he later reported proved sufficient to earn him a "B" in our modern poets class. Thanks to my friend, and even more to the Holy Spirit, this was the same final grade I also earned in "baby physics."

Two additional unforgettable grace events occurred much later in my adult life: Two weeks after the horror of the attacks on 9/11, I drove myself to the Emergency Department of the North Austin Regional Hospital. Once there, I reported my severe shortness of breath to the attending physician. After examining me for a few minutes, this physician called for a cardiologist. The cardiologist was quick to diagnose me with congestive heart failure and admitted me to the hospital.

As I lay in a bed in room 215 of the North Austin Regional Hospital, I spied a grackle perched on the outside stone sill of the only window in that room. I chuckled as I recalled that God had once sent ravens to feed Elijah, but for me, there was only a grackle. Within seconds, I fell into a trance of sorts when I was transported in my mind to the bed in the front bedroom of my grandparents' farm house in East Texas.

And in that mysterious moment, the year was 1956, and I was once again ten years old. As I stared out the window where once only a grackle rested, I could now see my Granddaddy's 1950 Chevrolet parked under the wide branches of three old post oaks. And in the silence of that mysterious moment, I knew that if my grandparents appeared in that window, I would climb out, and go with them wherever they had been summoned to take me.

But, of course, they didn't appear and a day or so later

I was released from the hospital with orders to report back in a week or so to undergo an echocardiogram of my heart. During the interim of that week, I decided I felt strong enough to keep an invitation to preach at a large Episcopal church in Austin.

The word of my illness had spread throughout the congregation, and following my sermon, a great number of well-wishers, all of whom assured me I was in their prayers, embraced me.

As I was making my exit from the church, a young woman approached me. Her entire being bespoke a piety grounded in the kind of sincerity I have found all too rare. Something so indefinable and special about her made me stop walking and pause to see what she might have to say. I suspected, and even hoped, she wanted to praise my imminently forgettable sermon, but instead she said, "You are sick, aren't you?"

Feeling somewhat red-faced, I said, "Yes, I'm sick."

"May I pray for you?"

Of course, I answered in the affirmative, thinking she would go home and get on her knees and pray. Instead she placed her hand on my forehead and prayed aloud on my behalf. Being a lifelong Presbyterian, I felt a bit uncomfortable. In our tradition, we don't touch much when we pray.

To be certain, some Arkansas Presbyterians laid their hands upon my balding head on the evening I was ordained, but that was about it, except for the day when I was only a few months old. Some pastor placed a hand full of water on my head in the name of the Father, and of the Son, and of the Holy Spirit.

The very next morning, I underwent the echocardiogram, and that afternoon the cardiologist called my home and left the following message on my voicemail: "Bob, you have been covered by grace. The echo shows your heart has returned to normal functioning."

After some questioning, the associate rector informed me that the woman who had prayed for me was a mystic, and, perhaps, even an angel, who served as the head of the church's healing ministry. She was also the founder of a small group known as "The Order of St. Luke."

Five years after my diagnosis of heart failure, I survived a cerebral hemorrhage otherwise known as a hemorrhagic stroke. After being transported to a hospital by helicopter, I awoke unable to open my eyes or swallow, or even walk. My thoughts were scrambled, and my entire left side was paralyzed.

I was blessed with a steady stream of visitors and well-wishers, all of whom informed me they were praying for me, but the simple, harsh reality was that I could not walk.

For that first full week in the hospital, I did my very best to follow the instructions of the dedicated physical therapist assigned to me. But as hard as I tried, and as focused as I forced myself to be, my left leg would not comply with the simple instructions of this most patient therapist. I hated disappointing him, but the stark truth was that I still could no longer walk.

As a kid, I had always loved playing whatever sport was in season, be it football, basketball or baseball. And as a young professional, I often ran a couple of miles at night in the inner city Dallas neighborhood where we lived.

But as I pulled myself into that hospital bed, I decided to face what I was certain had become my new reality. I would never walk again, much less run. I would not escort my daughter down the aisle at her wedding, and never again would I hike in the beautiful Rocky Mountains.

I thought of crying and feeling sorry for myself, but a tap on the door interrupted my self pity. Following my invitation to come in, two good friends appeared in the doorway. The first to enter was a true saint named Joe, and next came his colleague, Pablo.

Both of these fine gentlemen worked on the maintenance crew at the Austin mega-church where I served on the staff as teacher and pastoral counselor-in-residence. Joe's legendary kindness is exceeded only by his amazing competence. If it is broken, Joe can fix it. And if it needs building, Joe can not only build it, but he can also make it a thing of beauty and functionality.

Pablo is a quiet man with a pleasing baritone voice, who garners enormous respect through the art of demonstrating tranquility in every situation. While his work on the church maintenance crew was always first rate, I intuited that his many gifts were much more suited for the spiritual realm.

In fact, his nephew once confided in me that he was convinced his uncle was a healer. My typical reflex is to be skeptical of such claims, but when it came to Pablo, no such doubts emerged.

Although a bit tired, I was glad to see both of these good friends who, no doubt, had worked hard all day before making the effort to come see me in the hospital.

I'd no more shaken Joe's hand when Pablo whispered what sounded like a prayer.

I could not be certain if his petition was in English or Spanish, because my hearing was also affected by the stroke. But, of course, it made no difference because his words emerged from a pure heart, and when it comes to petitions sent to Heaven, purity matters.

Once he finished his prayer, this holy man removed a small glass container from his pants pocket and sprinkled some fine substance all over the left side of my body from my foot to my shoulder. Only later did he explain that it was dust lifted from a street in Jerusalem.

After Pablo concluded his prayer with a soft "Amen," both good friends bid me a goodnight, and I dropped off to sleep.

The next morning I awoke to the sound of my physical therapist's voice summoning me to attempt walking yet another time. As I slid out of bed, I realized I was standing on legs that felt strong enough to carry me the few precious steps all my previous efforts had failed to accomplish. Grinning like the Cheshire cat in Alice's Wonderland, the therapist took me by the arm and escorted me from the bed to the door, which was a full ten steps.

This good man turned to me. "Bob, you're walking."

I nodded, then requested permission to make a phone call. The therapist guided me back to the telephone, where I picked up the receiver and called Joe.

When Joe answered, I simply said, "Joe, I can walk. Thank you and thank Pablo for your prayers."

Two weeks later I was released from the hospital, and for the past fifteen years I've been walking pretty much whenever and wherever I please. And yes, I've even managed to hike on a few trails in Rocky Mountain National Park. But best of all, I was able to push a stroller containing the most precious cargo ever: my infant grandson, Henry, to whom this book is co-dedicated.

If I harbored any serious doubts regarding the efficacy of prayer, they were erased on the terribly sad morning in a Dallas hospital when I offered my father a final "goodbye." The illness attacking his heart left me no choice, and thus I was compelled to be there.

Once I exited his ICU room, I happened upon a small waiting area with only a single bench. My body dropped on that bench more than reclined on it. All I recall is burying my face in my arms and weeping. My sweet wife rushed to my side to inquire about my well-being.

I turned to her long enough to whisper, "I'm okay."

As always, her amazing intuition proved accurate, and she returned to the larger waiting room to give me time to myself.

Once more, I bowed my head and closed my eyes, but I could not think of the right words for any kind of prayer. Without warning, I heard a squeak followed by the sensation of someone breathing close to my face.

As I opened my tear-filled eyes, a baby boy, probably not yet a year old, stood in one of those "baby walkers" that roll wherever the child wishes to travel. As I struggled to focus, I realized that this little guy, who was no more than six inches from where my tears dropped to the floor, seemed curious about my demeanor.

He was a beautiful toddler with chubby rosy cheeks, a

grin that revealed a couple of tiny teeth, and enough drool covering his chin to qualify as a stream. His baby hair appeared to be as fine as corn silk and stuck straight up like some a startled cartoon character. And I was close enough to sniff a diaper in obvious need of immediate attention.

The baby's father rushed in to retrieve his "runaway son," and then to apologize for the child's intrusion upon my time alone.

I waved off the apology, and then thanked the man for allowing me to "visit" with his beautiful little boy, even if for only a few moments.

Of course, the young father appeared perplexed by my response, but my gratitude was heartfelt. This baby's unexpected interruption was a gift from Heaven.

One room away, my beloved father lay dying, while here before me stood a baby first sent to his parents and now to me by a loving God to proclaim the truth that in life as well as in death, the Almighty is always in control.

Life dies to this world before living forever in Heaven, and new life arrives to live full and meaningful lives, and our Heavenly Father is the Author of it all, and all of it is blessed.

Of course, the skeptics would say that the anecdotes presented above are mere examples of good fortune and/or coincidence. But when I gaze into the rearview mirror of my long life, I see an almost endless sequence of grace events, one following the other, and each one keeping my feet on the path my Heavenly Father had me travel.

So I don't waste either time or energy anymore trying to convince the skeptics.

No, I very simply say, "What's next?" And then I step out, waiting upon grace and walking in gratitude.

Chapter 4

The prayer Jesus taught us

World renowned reform theologian, Karl Barth, wrote: "To clasp hands in prayer is the beginning of the uprising against the disorder of the world." I did not even begin to appreciate the depth of this man's extraordinary insight until I took the time and made the effort to study the timeless words of Jesus that compose what we today know as The Lord's Prayer.

When I employ the word "study" here, by no means do I intend to suggest I'm any kind of biblical scholar. I am not now, nor have I ever achieved such a revered position within the church. No, I'm an ordinary man only one generation removed from the sharecropping class and culture of the tenant cotton farms of deep East Texas.

Furthermore, I possess no more than an average mind, if even that. I've long viewed myself as yet another unremarkable kid born into the "boomer generation," who was favored by the prodigious sacrifices of my wonderful mother and father to receive a very good education.

Because I was blessed to grow up in a vibrant and loving Presbyterian Church in a blue-collar section of Dallas, I learned to recite the words to The Lord's Prayer as a young child, and I prayed these words often and most of the time in unison with my peers, or in the context of worship with an entire congregation.

But like most folks, I prayed them for years without pausing to give any consideration whatsoever as to their meaning, much less to their requirements upon me as one who claims Jesus as Lord.

The sad truth is that most folks, both in the church and beyond, have prayed these words with such frequency and with such mindless nonchalance until they are inured not only to their meaning and power, but also to their revolutionary intent. This is true in my life, and I suspect it to be the case in the lives of most people today.

I once even heard of a high school football coach who had his team bow and recite the prayer before each game. However, before one especially important game, this man was so nervous to be facing his team's biggest rival, he instructed his players to take a knee and then led them in the Pledge of Allegiance.

And what struck me as so bizarre about this episode is that no one seemed to notice that this sacred prayer had in that moment morphed into a pledge to a flag and to the nation for which it stands.

As I mentioned above, I'm a scholar of absolutely nothing, and I've allowed all of the biblical Greek I learned more than 50 years ago to lie fallow too long. As a result, what you are about to read is a simple reflection, and nothing more than that, upon inarguably the most important prayer ever prayed.

What follows, then, is not at all an authoritative exegesis of this prayer, nor is it even an attempted explication of these holy words.

But because this is the prayer of Jesus, it deserves to be treated with a respect that approaches awe. And because I know my Heavenly Father to be a God of grace, and because I view Jesus as the living expression of God's very character, I dare to probe holiness with a profound sense of humility and respect for these words, and for what I take them to mean, as one who is more than willing to admit to his severe limitations.

After years of reciting this prayer in public worship as well as in my personal prayer time, I've come to believe that Jesus is summoning all who pray it—in the words of Barth—to rise up against the disorder of this world. To be clear, this is not a summons to join some new social movement or to vote a certain way, or to align ourselves with some charismatic political leader who points to the need for a wholesale revision of the status quo and then promises to lead us headlong into effecting that change.

No, this is something very different. It is a compelling summons for us to become the very kingdom Jesus came to proclaim.

Following his appropriate and beyond respectful salutation, Jesus enters into the prayer by asking for his Father's Kingdom to come to earth. And for the remainder of the prayer, he instructs his disciples, as well as us, how to join in the effort of bringing that Kingdom to full fruition.

Or, borrowing from Mahatma Gandhi, he summons us "to become the very change we seek." In simple terms, we are to become the kingdom as we join others in giving rise to a new spiritual revolution predicated upon Jesus' Beatitudes.

Let me explain further.

Right after Jesus' petition concerning the coming of this new kingdom, he informs us that the very fabric of this new order will be forever grounded in and determined by His Father's will. Thus, this Kingdom will turn our fallen world into a whole new reality very much resembling Heaven.

And how are we to accomplish this? Jesus directs us to keep our prayer requests simple by praying for our daily sustenance, as opposed to allowing our natural proclivity for longing for excess to contaminate our requests. This subtle injunction prevents us from launching into some ridiculous form of begging that we tell ourselves will satisfy our narcissistic appetite for prestige and/or power and for all the perks that attend these two insidious idols.

Next, he instructs us to forgive all who have wounded us, just as we have requested our Heavenly Father to forgive us for all of our wrongdoing. Either word we employ, trespasses or debts, is inconsequential, because both drive home the point that to be a part of this new Kingdom, we are to be steeped in the forgiveness business. Of course, this is not as easy as I make it sound, because all real forgiveness requires courage and the strength required to let go of all of our old resentments and to give up all grudges.

So, let us look closer at the structure of the prayer.

The salutation tells us a great deal. First, we learn Jesus regards God as the Father of us all. Jesus could instead have said, "My Father," thus viewing God as his exclusive kin. And this would not have been as far-fetched as it might sound at first. After all, if we believe in the doctrine of "the immaculate conception," it follows that Jesus could also make the claim for a one-of-a-kind kinship with God.

But he made no such claim. No, he very simply said, "Our Father," with his intention being clear: the Almighty is the one true God of the whole of humanity, regardless of ethnicity, nationality, or religious tradition.

Next, he informs us that God's place is in Heaven, which is something different from our earth. God's place, then, is other than our place.

The salutation concludes with the acknowledgment that God's name is holy. If you recall God's interface with Moses, you will, no doubt, remember that God tells Moses that his name is "I AM."

In ancient Israel, the name of God was considered so holy that it could never be spoken. Instead of "Yahweh," which was an approximation of the ancient Hebrew for "I AM," they substituted the word "Adonai," which means something like Lord, or my Lord.

But Jesus being the obedient Jew, he recognized that God's very name, along with everything else about God, was holy. And in ancient times as in today's world, that which is holy is set apart from all that is not holy, or in other words, from that which is profane.

In this succinct salutation, Jesus introduces us to a God who is like a loving Father to us, but who is at the same time holy and set apart from us. The implied tension between the images of an intimate and personally involved Father and a God whose intrinsic holiness sets Him apart from us is intentional. I suspect, it is given to us to remind us that intimacy with God is always a matter of recognizing the boundary separating our deepest longings from His abject holiness.

Following the salutation, Jesus goes to the very heart of the prayer by praying for God's Kingdom to come. And without taking a breath, he prays for the future to break into our present as he petitions his Father to make His holy will done right here on earth right now.

Simply put, he is praying for our fallen world to become like Heaven. The myriad implications are astounding here. A few of them are these:

*Genuine humble love will replace all other motives for human interaction.

*All wars will cease.

*Old enemies will become new friends.

*Kindness will become the normative ethos of every culture on earth.

*Across the entire globe, armed forces will disband, and defense budgets will shrink while new governmental budgets will become more geared to fund human health and educational programs.

*New economic opportunities, ones that will level the so-called playing field, will replace systemic poverty .

*The word for violence in every language will be deleted from the various dictionaries, the world over.

*Jails will be closed forever and prisons will be transformed into community colleges and/or trade schools.

*Divorce courts will close their doors and never reopen them.

*All drug cartels will dry up and blow away like dust.

*Domestic violence shelters will become neighborhood health care clinics.

*Politicians will at last become dedicated to the truth.

*Reconciliation will become normative in all human relationships.

*Hunger will be but a distant memory.

*The Earth's atmosphere will heal as our carbon footprint decreases to a great degree with each passing year.

*Guns will no longer be in the hands of any but law enforcement officers, and they will seldom, if ever, need to use them.

*Worship centers will be packed with people—whether Christian, Muslim, Jew, Hindu, or whatever—and those worshippers will be present every holy day for the purpose of offering heartfelt prayers of thanksgiving.

No doubt, most who read this list will think it so far-fetched as to be almost sophomoric, or worse, even silly. That said, what I've listed above are but a few possible examples of what I envision when Jesus' new kingdom comes to full fruition, and at long last, it is on earth as it is in Heaven.

For me, this is not some pie-in-the sky fantasy, but rather the possible, and even prophesied, result of a world turned on to the power of God to save us even from our own self-obsession.

I suspect that most who pray this prayer never pause to ponder the spiritual revolution for which they seem to be praying with such earnestness. And because most of us are hardwired to resist change, even that change which improves the quality of life the world over for all people, I sometimes wonder how often this prayer would be offered if folks considered its radical intentions.

While still in my twenties, I accepted a pastoral position on a large downtown church. And in my first year in that position, I collaborated with an older and much wiser pastor to found a soup kitchen to feed the homeless.

Needless to say, there was great consternation in the church following the opening of this new ministry in an unused space that had once been a small underground staff parking garage. By God's grace, that ministry has survived and even flourished for close to fifty years, and at last count had served over eight million meals.

But getting the thing up and running was no easy task. One of the leaders in the church confronted me in a church hallway one Sunday morning just weeks after the opening of the soup kitchen.

Her tone was angry and her eyes were on fire with a rage I'd not experienced before, at least not in person. Scowling like a mule chomping on prickly pear she said, "What do you mean, bringing bums and winos in this church? They are filthy human beings, and we don't want them here."

As she paused to catch a breath, I dared to say, "So, what is it you do want?"

Her scowl never softened as she said, "You've been brought here to teach us about Jesus."

The irony in this response was lost on her, but I came dangerously close to chuckling. We founded the entire program because it was the very Jesus about whom she wanted us to teach her who once said, "In as much as you have done it to the least of these, you have done it to me."

And as best I could tell, the couple of hundred homeless men and women who showed up every day to receive their "daily bread" certainly qualified as Jesus' "least of these." And even though I was young, inexperienced, and terribly naïve, I thought that modeling Jesus as best we could was an effective method in teaching others not only about his ministry, but also about his mission here on earth.

Years later this woman and I became good friends, and she even became a big supporter of the soup kitchen, which we named, "the Stewpot."

The more I ponder this radical nature of this simple prayer, the more I believe we human beings also disregard what it requires of us, because becoming a citizen of the kingdom Jesus proclaimed asks a high price. The core truth is that it costs us our very way of being the person we've always been.

And when I remember the resistance I encountered by launching a few programs aimed at feeding and sheltering the "least of these," I recognize just how easy it is to relegate this prayer either to the rank of some kind of pious little talisman or to its even lesser significance as the preamble to a meeting or as the prelude to the controlled violence we call football.

But in the church, as well as in the world at large, it is high past time to recognize this prayer for what it has been for the past two millennia—and for what it is today—a summons, issued by Jesus himself, to join the Holy Spirit in bringing Heaven to Earth, right here and right now.

Such a concept is too much for us to contemplate, much less accept, so we neither consider nor accept it as we recite the words and then move on to whatever comes next. And what does come next is the petition for us to receive our daily bread.

As I mentioned above, this request remains simple and unencumbered by any additional requests for creature comforts or for certain circumstances to break in our favor. No, this petition is about our sustenance served on a daily basis. In other words, we are getting a lesson in praying for sufficient sustenance to stay alive, and that's about it.

Once we receive that, we can then move on to the next

part of the prayer, which calls us to get started with the business of forgiveness.

Forgiving others is difficult, but perhaps the most challenging part of this work is to forgive ourselves. Serving as a pastoral counselor for 25 years, I invested hundreds of hours inviting and even encouraging folks to forgive themselves of their sins. Most could, with some effort and with no small amount of encouragement on my part, and at last did, in time, come to forgive themselves.

However, I do remember one young beautiful woman, a newlywed whose ceremony was held in our church sanctuary. Mere weeks following that memorable, "storybook ceremony," she called to request an appointment.

Our initial session together was marked by a river of tears, shoulder shaking sobs, and only enough enunciation on her part to inform me that she was convinced God hated her.

Several sessions and more sobs later, I came to learn that she had as a young college freshman become pregnant by her first real boyfriend. To hide her shame, and to escape responsibilities for which she was not prepared, she sought an abortion. In her mind, she had committed the unforgivable sin.

I did everything I'd been taught to convince her that because God is a God of grace, she was forgiven. I prayed with her, I quoted Scripture, focusing on St. Paul's Letter to the Romans, and most specifically where the apostle writes that nothing "will be able to separate us from the love of God in Jesus Christ." *(Romans 8:39b)*

At times, I felt as though I was performing an "exorcism" of sorts in my futile attempt to cast out the toxic demon, neurotic guilt. But the more I persisted, the more she resisted. Nothing I tried worked with this woman. Absolutely nothing.

In her view, she had willfully committed an unforgiveable sin, and not one attempt on my feeble part could convince her otherwise. I suspect, she clung to some tiny sliver of hope, because she kept coming to see me. But each session accomplished nothing more than to reinforce our impasse.

As time went by, I prepared to hand her off to someone else, which I recognized was not at all right, but it was either that or allow her to live as best she could, holding on to her unnecessary burden of guilt.

One afternoon when I was walking my fat, old English bull dog, Stonewall Jackson Lively, in the inner city neighborhood where we lived, it dawned on me that while she had converted intellectually to the Protestant faith in order to please her new husband, her emotions still very much bound her to the culture of the faith into which she had been raised.

She was emotionally still very much a Catholic.

What she needed was absolution, and I didn't qualify for that particular task, so the very next morning I called a friend who was a Catholic priest and requested that he hear her confession. This was an audacious decision on my part, because I was the one who had "robbed" the Catholics of one of their lambs, but I knew this priest well, a gentle soul who not only exuded grace, but also expressed a very strong interest in ecumenism.

He agreed to see this woman, and at our next session I assured her there was no way I was giving up on her, but rather I was interested in trying a whole new approach. With some reluctance, she agreed and then called the priest from my office to schedule the confession.

This presented no great risk on my part, because I knew this man would rather have cut off one of his own fingers with a rusty blade than to shame or scold this woman for what she perceived to be her unforgivable sin. Some days later she returned to my office smiling and bearing a much lighter countenance.

When I inquired as to her experience with the priest, I saw her grin for the very first time. And then with a sigh that ushered in more tears to roll down her face, she said, "The priest listened carefully and patiently while I sobbed and sobbed. Finally, I managed to get it all out, and that's when he surprised me by telling me that my penance was done. The priest said, 'The terrible suffering you have experienced by holding on to your guilt is your penance. And you have held on for too long, so it's time to give it to Christ.'

'But will he take it?'

"The priest said, 'He took it centuries ago on that terrible day when Rome nailed him to a cross. And he took it from you and kept it to himself because he loves you far more than you can even imagine. And now do as Jesus once admonished another young girl—this one accused of adultery—"go your way, and from now on do not sin again".' *(John 8:11b)*

"Before I left the confessional, I said, 'Is that it?'

" 'What more could there possibly be?' the priest said, and with that, I did as he said, and I went home feeling like a new woman."

Perhaps less difficult is the forgiveness toward those who have wounded us deeply. At least, in my clinical experience it tends to be so. Jesus tells us that we are to "pray for those who persecute us." *(Matthew. 5:44)*

And this simple admonishment is the only way to experience any genuine inner peace, even in the wake of being severely wounded. All of us get hurt in our lives, with no exceptions. We get shamed, ridiculed, rejected, humiliated, bullied, discounted, or far worse. In fact, one of my mentors was fond of saying, "No one gets into adulthood unscathed." We all have scars, and as a result, we all have issues which cry out for resolution.

And, like it or not, the only way to resolve those issues is to pray for those who have hurt us.

In the first year of my clinical residency in pastoral counseling, I was assigned to co-lead an evening group with a lovely young woman named Cathy. Cathy was bright, experienced, and credentialed while I was a yet-to-be-certified neophyte.

We worked together several weeks together before she deigned to share with me her story one night following our group session. She told me that she was single, because her husband, who was a successful physician, had had an affair. But what struck me as the most important facet to her story was the "secret" she had discovered in finding her way back to a serene, and even joyful life.

As a devout Catholic, she knew she must forgive her

ex-husband, who had wounded her far more deeply the she thought might ever be possible. She told me that she never came to the point of hating him but that she did hate what he had done to her dreams of a long and happy life with him.

With the help of her therapist, she began a discipline where she prayed for her ex-husband to enjoy great success and to experience genuine happiness in his life. And she told me that, of course, the most difficult challenge in this new prayer discipline was to remain sincere.

Once she achieved the desired sincerity, she prayed for her ex-husband's well-being every night for two weeks. She reported that following that two-week discipline, a minor miracle occurred. Her rage subsided to a significant degree and her bitterness all but disappeared.

I've never been betrayed like this woman was, but I have been so deeply wounded that I seriously considered leaving the ministry for which I'd invested so many years of my life in training. For too many years, I languished in bitterness and resentment.

At long last, I convinced myself to try the discipline of praying for those cruel ones who had tossed me out of the church. For two full weeks I prayed for distinct blessings for all the folks who had so wounded me and my family.

And after those two weeks, the bitterness lifted, and the resentment fell away, and I felt like a new man who was now ready to reinvent myself within the context of the ministry.

At this point, I will say here what I've said to scores of people over the course of my ministry: This prayer business really works, but it only if you really work it, and by working it, I mean that one must pray with a sincere heart.

Or, as Mark Twain put it so succinctly in his classic *Huckleberry Finn*, "You cannot pray a lie."

The final part of Jesus' prayer is the petition asking God to deliver us from the temptations of the evil one. St. Matthew's version reads:

"And do not bring us to the time of trial, but rescue us from the evil one." *(Matthew 6:9)*

Many folks who pray this prayer stumble over this petition in that (1) they cannot imagine a God, who is absolute love, bringing anyone to the time of trial, and (2) they don't want to know or to have any commerce whatsoever with the evil one.

So, what does Jesus mean by including this final petition?

To address this question, we must first identify the evil one.

His earliest appearance in Scripture came in the ancient etiological myth the Hebrews either created themselves and /or borrowed from other cultures to explain the whole of creation. In essence, the story was about God's created perfection being forever contaminated by the evil one whose sole purpose is to lie. And early on in Scripture, he assumes the form of a serpent for the purpose of lying to our spiritual ancestors, and, thereby forever contaminating God's perfect garden.

The evil one's core message was this: you cannot trust God.

And the very strong implication that follows was this: you must instead trust in yourself, and in your own wits, and your own power to persuade others to your point of view and ultimately control your world as you see fit.

In its simplest, most insidious, form the message was this: God is a liar.

Hence, you must become the ruler of your own life.

And because our spiritual ancestors proved themselves incapable of discernment, and because they listened to the evil one's lies, and far worse, embraced those lies as truth, humankind was forever cast out of God's perfectly ordered garden.

Of course, this etiological myth is not a representation of any anthropological reality, and yet, it is rife with the amazing truth that our fundamental problem as human beings is grounded in our strong proclivity for trusting in ourselves as opposed to placing our trust in God.

Years ago, I was counseling a young woman who was terrified that her son, a recently enrolled university student, would not be successful in his studies due to some learning disorders.

I felt her pain as she sat before me crying. At last, I said, "What can you do about all of this?"

When she raised her eyes to meet mine, she said, "Nothing."

"I respectfully disagree."

"Yeah," she said. "What can I do?"

"You can give him to God."

She bowed her head and clinched both fists and waited. I didn't know what her response might be, whether anger, or rage or, perhaps, curiosity.

After a few moments, she lifted her countenance to me

one more time, and this time she smiled. "But what if God doesn't know what he's doing?" she said before her laughter disallowed any addendum to her question.

After I laughed with her, I said, "Then we're all screwed."

And we ended our time together on that note.

Of course, the incontrovertible truth here is that God does know what He is doing. That is why Jesus trusted him with everything, even with his life and his horrendous death upon a Roman cross.

But it is the goal of the evil one is to make us so doubt God's involvement in our lives that over time we come to rely upon ourselves even to the point of viewing ourselves as the sole executive of our own unique life circumstances. Without question, we all have to make important choices every day, but the wisest among us have learned to view those decisions always through the prism of God's holy will for their lives.

So why does Jesus instruct us to pray that we might not be brought to the time of trial? Perhaps, the most obvious reason is that Jesus had been driven by the Spirit into the wilderness where he fasted for forty days and for forty nights.

And because of his self-deprivation, he weakened himself on purpose, which made him vulnerable. The evil one who showed up, peddling the same lie he used with our spiritual ancestors to get them evicted from God's perfect Order.

Jesus knows we're not up to such a trial, so he instructs us to pray. Then we might be spared the ordeal he experienced in the wilderness once the evil one appeared to him.

The purpose of such an encounter was to convince Jesus to abandon forever his mission of bringing God's kingdom to earth.

With the crucifixion, the evil one appeared to win, but God had the final word in the resurrection.

The remainder of the prayer, known as the doxological portion, has long been the topic of debate regarding its authorship. This portion concludes the prayer as follows:

"For Thine is the Kingdom, and the Power, and the Glory forever and ever. Amen."

Some scholars believe that this portion of the prayer was interpolated by an unknown editor(s) into the prayer some centuries after Jesus. I don't know if this is true. But this squabble is irrelevant to me, because as I child, I learned to include the doxological portion as an appropriate conclusion. And today I see no reason to omit it, even if it did not originate with Jesus.

And in the final analysis, it does nothing to detract from the prayer, but to the contrary, I see this brief statement of praise as the most fitting way to conclude this radical prayer before we say, "Amen."

Chapter 5

The transformative power of prayer

All of us stand in need of some form of transformation, be it ever so minor, or a full scale redo of our very soul. The reason for this is simple. All of us are born into imperfect families.

As a result, all of us live with and do the best we can with some form of psychopathology.

For some folks, such as those raised in highly dysfunctional families, the ego defenses are so pronounced as to become serious issues—e.g., personality disorders. For others who were raised with far less dysfunction, the disorders are not as serious and can be treated within the context of both uncovering and supportive psychotherapy.

One of my greatest discoveries in my two-year clinical residency in a pastoral counseling training program was that I was introduced to a great number of folks who were suffering as adults due to the tragedy of being abused as children. I walked away from that intensive two years more convinced than ever that this world is full of pain and all manner of suffering.

As a pastor in a large inner city church, I never realized neither the depth nor the ubiquity of human suffering. And the primary reason I failed to see this was because most people tend to put their best foot forward when they attend worship. But whether or not it was visible to me or to others, their pain was always present, simmering beneath a fragile patina of piety and friendliness.

As I read the Epistles of St. Paul, and as I read about him in the words of his biographer, St. Luke, I wonder what his formative years must have been like. From what we know about him, he was born to parents, who were Jews and, at the same time, Roman citizens in the ancient city of Tarsus.

Tradition tells us his parents likely moved to Jerusalem some time while he was still a child, thus affording Saul the opportunity to be exposed to the greatest Jewish scholars and rabbis of his time. From what we know of Saul, written by his own hand, is that he was gifted intellectually.

He put it this way:" I advanced in Judaism beyond many of the young people of the same age." *(Galatians 1:14)*

No doubt, Saul was the valedictorian of his class of pharisaical students. He was the best and the brightest among his peers, and he not only knew it, he also embraced his intellectual gifts as a way to gain status, or if you will, to climb the career ladder in his chosen profession as a Pharisee.

This minor exhibition of narcissism concerns me not in the least, because all of us enjoy speaking of our own accomplishments and their attendant accolades. What, of course, concerns me is this statement:

"I was violently persecuting the church of God and trying to destroy it." *(Galatians 1:13)*

The question that has longed dogged me concerns the problem of Saul's pathological obsession with his religion. While I view faithfulness and piety as a good thing, any obsession that drives us to destroy others is invariably pathological.

And in my clinical experience, any form of religious obsession is often an ego defense far more than it is a true expression of faith and/or piety. People dealing with issues they view as ego-dystonic, or that is, wholly unacceptable, sometimes resort to being overly zealous in the attempt to hide from their repressed guilt by becoming obnoxious crusaders for God.

When we first encounter Saul, Luke tells of him being present while a mob stones to death a man named Stephen. In fact, the men who stoned this martyr laid their coats at Saul's feet while they went about their murderous work of destroying a man whose only crime was that he dared to speak the truth of Jesus Christ. *(Acts 7:54F)*

If Saul, the gifted young Pharisee, experienced any compunction whatsoever to put a stop to the horror now unfolding before him, he never acted upon it. No, he stood by dispassionately and watched a man die a horrible death at the hands of a crazed mob who believed they were wholly justified in murdering anyone who held a different view of God than their own.

And Luke tells us that this man Saul approved of the

mob's slaughter of a man who dared to preach a new and very different revelation of God. Stephen was willing to die for his faith, while Saul continued to increase his rabid determination to put an end to this new movement which was fast becoming known as "the people of the way."

Two chapters later, in Chapter 9 of Acts, Saul appears again, and this time Luke paints a picture his of zeal as more fiery than ever, as he is described as "breathing threats and murder against the disciples of the Lord." *(Acts 9:1)*

Saul is no longer satisfied to be a mere witness to the public execution of a man who committed no real offense. No, now he had devolved into a man willing, and even eager, to defend his version of the faith by whatever means necessary, including murder. This is sociopathy in its most florid form. Saul's apparent narcissistic disorder has at this point obviously devolved into full-blown sociopathy.

Today most Christians believe they know the rest of the story that goes something like this:

• Saul visits with the chief priest in order to secure letters to the synagogues in Syria. Of course, his purpose is to investigate the members of these synagogues. And if he finds any folks embracing this new way of believing, he plans to tie them up against their will and haul them back to Jerusalem, where, most likely their fate will be the same as Stephen's.

• But, of course, Jesus himself interrupted Saul's vengeful mission, first appearing as a flash of blinding light, then saying to him, "Saul, Saul, why do you persecute me?" *(Acts 9:5)*

Now blinded by the light, Saul asks the voice to identify himself.

• His traveling companions led Saul into the city of Damascus, where he remains blind and where he takes no food nor drink for three days. At last, an obedient man, who has been instructed by the Holy Spirit to go to Saul, finds Saul and lays his hands upon him. Saul not only sees again, but he is now filled with the Holy Spirit.

• At this point, Saul decides to use his Roman (or Latin) name, Paul, as he begins his new ministry of preaching the truth that Jesus is the long-awaited Messiah.

And most folks believed this was a quick conversion lasting only no more than a few days. This version goes as follows: Saul is blinded by a light and hears a voice and then becomes the apostle to the Gentiles, as he journeys westward, preaching Jesus, founding churches, and forever altering the course of Western civilization.

But as we return to Paul's Letter to the Church at Galatia, we read more details regarding his post-conversion life. He tells us that he did not confer with any other human beings, nor did he seek the counsel of the apostles who remained in Jerusalem.

Instead, he traveled to Arabia before returning to Damascus. In all, this journey into his own soul required three years. And during the whole of those three years, he provides no concrete information as to how he spent his time.

That said: An educated guess would suggest that he most likely invested the lion's share of his time praying and listening to the Holy Spirit regarding further instructions. And it was during this three-year span that the transformation of his mind, soul, and spirit were healed of all hatred. For the first time in his life, he became a whole human being.

I make this claim for two reasons:

One, throughout his letters he admonishes new believers to pray, even to the point of instructing the folks at Thessalonica "to pray without ceasing." *(1 Thessalonians.5:17-19)*

And two, it is at this point in his writing that he tells of his discovery of the dichotomy within himself as well as within the whole of humanity. Here, he characterizes that dichotomy in pre-Freudian language as the choice one has either to live in the flesh or to live in the Spirit.

More simply put, we can live either for ourselves and for our ego-gratification, or we can live for that Someone far greater than ourselves, which most call God.

I am quite willing to posit here that when Paul writes of this dichotomy, he is writing his autobiography. This is not some abstract theory or new psycho/spiritual pre-scientific speculation. No, this is Paul writing about his own transformation in the most humble way he knows how.

He no longer feels the need to boast of his brilliance and of the fact that among his peers he was the best and the brightest. He is a transformed man who now recognizes perhaps for the first time in his life that, for his thirty-plus years of living, he has operated entirely out of "the flesh," or what today we post-Freudian people would call the ego.

Paul now sees that he has lived only for himself and has thereby pursued interests for his own personal benefit. And in his twisted way of thinking, he suspected that if he could only nip in the bud this new movement dedicated to the Lordship of Jesus, he could enjoy his next half century as a highly respected, and perhaps even famous, Pharisee, and thus reap the rewards of one being so highly regarded.

But Paul is now a changed man, and he wants his audience to know what the Spirit has done for him. And yet, he realizes he cannot boast, although his passion is unmistakable as he communicates the vast difference between his former life in the flesh and his new life in the Spirit. This is no easy task, but he pulls it off by presenting his discovery of the dichotomy in abstract terms.

When Paul writes of the "fruit of the Spirit," he is telling the world of the amazing gifts he, himself, has received from the Holy Spirit. Note that he doesn't go to Arabia for three years and invest both his time and his life energy choosing to become a better man.

No, there is far more to this story than a mere decision on the part of a sociopath to somehow become an improved human being. It doesn't work that way. These amazing new qualities are what he clearly describes as "fruit." And this fruit comes to him as a result of prayer.

I suspect that following his encounter with Jesus on the road to Damascus, Paul experienced a near spirit-breaking load of guilt. And furthermore, he realized he would need to be made whole before he could hope even to begin his mission of becoming an apostle to the Gentiles.

Of course, being a First Century man, he didn't know to view himself as a sociopath, but such was his disorder, at least from the time he stood by and watched a mob stone poor Stephen to death.

Therefore, it is not at all far-fetched to imagine that he asked the Holy Spirit for help, and the Holy Spirit responded by blessing him with what again Paul described to the Galatians as "the fruit of the Spirit". *(Galatians5:22)*

And the fruit of the Spirit is love, patience, kindness, generosity, faithfulness, gentleness, and self-control. *(Galatians 5:22-23)*

It's very plain that these qualities represent the very antithesis of sociopathy. But, by the time he writes his letter to the Galatians, these qualities have become accurate descriptors of both his character and his personality.

Therefore, I believe that what Paul is telling the Church at Galatia is that through prayer and by the Holy Spirit he has been made whole.

Am I suggesting here that one can pray himself/herself out of sociopathy? Yes, that is what I am saying with this one caveat:

The one who seeks the kind of radical transformation Paul experienced will stand in need of guidance and supervision by one who is wise, seasoned, and, most of all, whole.

Too often, we minimize the power of prayer to transform us and ultimately heal us from the person we made ourselves to be. We have a hard time believing we can be changed into the person God created us to be in His image.

In my brief career as a chaplain in a drug and alcohol recovery center, I taught classes in contemplative prayer. I started by inviting my students to assume a relaxed position in a chair or on the floor. Once they signaled they were ready to pray by raising their hands, I invited them to focus on the words I lifted from Scripture.

My two favorites were:

"Be still and know that I am God." *(Psalm 46:10)*

and

"God is love." *(1st John 4:8)*

The results of teaching this discipline exceeded my expectations because after each class, students in both the men's and women's units sought me out to tell me how much this discipline of praying Scripture had proved beneficial to them and to their recovery.

One man even told me that he gave up on his recovery. One night he packed his few belongings into a paper sack, then hiked more than three miles to the closest bus stop where he caught a bus bound for downtown Austin.

He said that somewhere on that bus ride, the words, "God is love," came to him, and he decided to ride the bus all the way back to the very place where he had caught it an hour before. At that point, he abandoned the bus and returned to treatment.

Some few years later, I was enjoying breakfast one

Saturday morning in a restaurant in central Austin. Sitting alone in a booth, I was aware of someone hovering behind me. I turned to see a vaguely familiar face smiling at me.

The young man who belonged to that face said, "God is love."

As he sat across from me in the booth, he told me he had worked at this small restaurant for about two years where he sometimes waited tables and sometimes worked as a line cook. He was eager to tell me that while he was riding the bus that fateful night in his attempt to escape recovery, he decided he would find no love mixing with the drug dealers and pimps in downtown Austin. Furthermore, he reported that he'd remained clean and sober from the first day of his release from treatment until the present.

To the Holy Spirit goes the glory, and of course, the credit for this man's recovery from in Paul's words, a life in the flesh to a new life in the Spirit.

The discipline of praying Scripture is an ancient Catholic practice known as "Lectio Divina," or more commonly known today as centering prayer. I've not only read of its effectiveness as a tool for spiritual healing, but also I've witnessed it firsthand.

When all is said and done, I'm convinced the Holy Spirit could work miracles if the politicians and penologists could ever figure out a way to lower the wall separating church and state long enough for the chaplains to teach inmates how to pray their way to wholeness.

Chapter 6

Too deep for words...

There are times in every person's experience when life takes us to the depths. Here, I do not intend to suggest that the term 'depths' points exclusively to negative experiences, such as despair, desolation, despondency, depression, or grief.

No, what I intend is to point toward those uncommon and extraordinarily poignant moments where something happens to us, and/or for us, and all attempts at explanation appear superficial, and all reflexive shallow answers prove useless.

Any number of forces can take us to such a place, and a few of them are such drivers as fatigue, hopelessness, anxiety, frustration, an overwhelming sense of betrayal, confusion, grief, or perhaps even an amazing one-on-one surprise encounter with Holiness. But whatever the driver, it plumbs the depths of our souls with such force and with such power as to render us speechless and unable even to pray

Again, in his letter to the Church at Rome, Paul writes of his own subjective experience when he assures us that "the Spirit helps us in our weakness; for we do not know how to pray as we ought, but that very Spirit intercedes with sighs too deep for words." *(Romans 8:26)*

There have been several moments in my life when I was compelled to journey to the very depths of my being as I searched for the path toward wholeness.

One such time occurred during my final semester in college when I developed a case of insomnia. For the life of me, I could not sleep. Nothing I tried seemed to work. I ran laps on the track around the football field, I joined two good friends in driving ten miles to another town where the sale of beer was legal, and I even went so far as to purchase some harmless over-the-counter sleeping aides in the college book store. But nothing worked.

In a century-old dormitory, each night I lay awake in a small bunk where I worried about going to Vietnam either to kill other men or to be killed and then shipped home in a box to be buried somewhere by my grieving family. I brooded over escaping to Canada in order to hide from the draft. Somehow this route felt like a betrayal of the country I loved.

So night after night, I lay wide awake, even more exhausted than the night before, as I tossed and turned, and as I told myself that my four years of study had been in vain. As far as I was concerned, I had no future whatsoever. All I could see before me was death, the death of a dream and the death of other men, and, of course, my own death.

What I was too ill-informed and far too naïve to realize was that I could have sought help at the campus health center. But of course I didn't do that. Instead, by placing the whole of my dread squarely upon my own shoulders, I suffered.

And, most important, what I failed to recognize was that help was available to me all along, laid out to me and to the ages, beautifully in the eighth chapter of St. Paul's letter to the Church at Rome.

All I knew in those painful days was that I could not sleep and neither could I speak what I regarded as any kind of meaningful prayer. I tried to pray, but I could not find any words other than the word "Help!"

But that didn't seem to be sufficient, at least not enough to make me consider it any kind of more substantive prayer. But that one-word prayer was all I could manage.

What I didn't know—and was perhaps too lazy to discover on my own—is that I was never alone with this sense terrible sense of dread and worry. Through it all, the Holy Spirit who loved me far more than I could ever imagine was interceding for me with sighs too deep for words. I didn't know to listen for those sighs.

In retrospect, I'm now certain they were present and sent to comfort me by a loving God who had plans for me that were far better than anything I could envision on my own.

At this point in his life, Paul has matured to the point where he is both able and empowered by his own subjective faith development to write about a unique mystical experience, one I describe as genuine and personal intimacy with God. And within the context of this intimacy, he hears the Holy Spirit praying on his behalf with sighs that are so deep and so profound as to transcend all words.

And his most amazing message to us, his readers, is that this same intimacy and divine intervention is available to all of us. His astounding proclamation is this: When we're unable to pray for ourselves, the Spirit intercedes on our behalf, and our Heavenly Advocate actually prays for us.

If there is better news than this anywhere in Paul's writings, I cannot guess what it might be. Here, we not only receive permission to become mystics, but we are also assured God is always for us and God is always intimately involved in our individual, and seemingly ordinary, lives.

Had I been sufficiently wise or mature to embrace Paul's take on intimacy with God when I was a 21-year-old college senior, I would have gladly swapped worry for sleep and the sum of my dread for joy. Plus I lacked genuine literacy in the Word to know to embrace the truth of the abject uselessness of worry.

By far, the most poignant moment in my prayer life occurred following my goodbye to a congregation I had served for more than a full decade. Without question, this was the most painful chapter in both my professional and personal life.

In my mind, I had served this congregation with distinction even to the point of being recognized in a formal resolution by the Mayor of Dallas for my decades-long work of relieving the suffering of the city's homeless population. And only a year prior to my dismissal, the Governor of Texas had invited me to Austin to be recognized for my work with the homeless.

But the congregation I served called a new senior pastor to lead the church, and because tremendous anxiety is always attached to any such transition, some (but not all) of the church lay leadership made it abundantly clear that it was time for me to move on. The way I saw it, this new senior pastor was entitled to choosing his own staff, and, of course, that group would not include me.

This man was gifted and at least kind to a superficial degree; however, he had never served a church before. And most important, he and I shared very different world views.

From the first day I met him, he appeared close to be obsessed with increasing the size of the congregation, and, thereby soothing the collective angst in the church leadership in assuring that this old downtown congregation would survive into the coming Twenty-First Century.

And while I agreed with him that evangelism was, indeed, important, I viewed my mission as that of guiding our members in their spiritual growth through participating in the incarnational life of the church as the risen body of Christ. He and I worked together for a few months and we seemed to establish a working relationship that was, at least functional.

However, in the late summer of his first year, everything came to a head when I was offered two wonderful opportunities I didn't believe I could turn down.

The first was to write a history of a revered Presbyterian church conference center located in the Texas Hill Country, and the second was to teach a course in "Community Ministry" at my alma mater, Austin Presbyterian Theological Seminary in Austin, Texas. Of course, I wanted to accept both invitations, but I knew I couldn't do that without permission from this new senior pastor and the personnel committee.

As a result, I submitted a written request to take a three-month "sabbatical" in order to write the book. And I asked for permission to change my day off from Friday to Monday so I could fly to Austin each week to teach at the seminary.

In my ten years of service to this church, I'd never asked these people for anything. In fact, I'd worked every holiday except Christmas Day to keep the soup kitchen operating. And during my last five years of service, I even worked on Saturdays, supervising the Bible school format we provided every Saturday morning for some of the most deprived children in all of Dallas, Texas.

Therefore, I didn't view it at all out of order to make these two requests to the new guy and to his small circle of leaders.

But, of course, both requests were denied.

Then I did what the small circle of leaders and the new pastor wanted me to do. I resigned.

And in the wake of this difficult decision, I received numerous messages from my fellow Presbyterians informing me I had just committed professional suicide. I couldn't argue with them because I knew they were right. Since we don't have bishops or anyone else, for that matter, to help us find new positions, we were instructed early on in our seminary training to never, never resign a position without having somewhere else to go.

I've never in my life felt more vulnerable or more alone, and yet, I could not come up with of any other course. My thinking was this: If I had killed all future opportunities in the Presbyterian Church, so be it. I would become a secondary school teacher and invest the remainder of my life teaching kids and writing books.

By resigning, I was able to buy myself six more months' time, and these months afforded me the opportunity to accept the seminary's invitation to teach the class. Further, this interim period gave me time to research the conference center's history that I planned to write that summer.

At last, my designated departure date arrived, and I preached my final sermon. Much to my surprise, even astonishment, the congregation gave me a standing ovation following that very forgettable sermon.

I've never allowed myself to believe the motives underlying that ovation had anything at all to do with that sermon, but I suspect it was a mixture of some tepid appreciation for my work, along with a collective sense of relief that I would be gone and forever done with challenging these people to consider new and better ways to serve the poor.

That evening, a true saint invited my family and me to her beautiful home to join with the very small group of folks she knew appreciated me. I felt torn during that little party, because I was grateful to be finished forever with the difficult work serving in this church, and yet, I hated saying goodbye to the few truly good friends I'd managed to make in that congregation.

And hanging over my head like the sword of Damocles was the dread of facing tomorrow with neither employment nor any real prospects.

With the perfunctory little party over, I did my best to

remain cheerful as my wife and ten-year-old daughter and I returned home. That night, as I tucked my daughter into her little bed, I fought back the tears. And for the very first time in her life, I had no ready answers as to how I would provide for her without a job. If she was worried, she never showed it. She reached for me to offer her final hug of the day followed by her typical goodnight kiss.

No sooner had I tucked her in bed for the last time that night than the first rumble of thunder cracked. Its roar was so deep and protracted, almost with the certainty that something threatening was fast approaching the city. Blinding flashes of lightning filled her tiny bedroom, so frightening that our beloved old bulldog, Stonewall Jackson Lively, whimpered from his usual hiding place beneath my daughter's bed.

I reached for Jackson's collar as I did every night at bedtime, and like always, I gave thought to taking him to the backyard for a night of peaceful slumber beneath the stars. But no stars were shining on this night, only thunder, and flashes of fire, followed by torrents of rain. Not at all certain as to my next move, I pulled open the back door and found our entire yard flooded in several inches of water.

Jackson remained reticent as I coaxed him onto the small stoop that was the closest thing we could claim as any kind of back porch. And for no good reason other than the fact that I enjoy watching storms, I joined Jackson on that small concrete stoop where we were protected from the rain by a thin sheet of fiberglass above our heads.

And there we remained for several minutes as the stormed raged its fury and as the evening rolled inexorably

toward what I had long dreaded, a new day with zero prospects for meaningful employment.

I wrapped one arm around Jackson's thick neck as I
whispered to him, and even more to myself, words of reas-
surance I knew rang hollow.

I suspect Jackson also sensed I was lying to both of us,
because I was in no way certain what negative consequences
my decision would have on what had begun as a promising
career. Jackson was good enough to pretend to listen as I
rambled on while the storm above us raged.

Then just as suddenly as it had fired up, the storm fell
strangely silent, as even the wind obeyed a command to
hold its fury for a few seconds. And, in that moment, it was
as if the entire night had paused to sigh.

This time I spoke to my dog what I knew to be the
truth: "We're going to be okay."

To this day, I still don't know how I came to discover
the truth on that memorable night in a North Texas thun-
derstorm, but somehow I managed to discern a sigh deeper
than even thunder, and in that unexpected, albeit brief,
silence I knew Someone, somewhere was praying for me.

And following that discovery, I knew worry was what it
always is, a waste of time. I slept soundly until the morning
arrived. I awoke to the truth that the storm was done with
us.

Chapter 7

"For we do not know how to pray..."

Romans 8:26

My first pastorate was to serve as the first-ever campus minister at a tiny Presbyterian college nestled in the foothills of Arkansas' version of the Ozarks. My primary duties focused on meeting the spiritual needs of students, most of whom were from the backwoods villages and hamlets that dotted the mountains and hollows of Northern Arkansas. I offered a worship service in a small campus chapel to a handful of faithful students, three of whom went on to enter seminary and later become ordained into the Presbyterian Church, USA.

But most of all, my work consisted of walking around the campus and interacting with students to form relationships. The rest of my time was spent in my office, where I listened to students talk to me about everything, from their relationship issues to their vocational dreams.

It was a good place for one as raw and as untested

as myself to begin a career in pastoral ministry, because the challenges were minimal and any big controversies nonexistent.

However, all sense of serenity evaporated one day following a call from this tiny school's athletic department. The voice on the other end requested I write and then record a prayer that could be offered over a public address system prior to the initial jump ball of each game in the annual North Arkansas small high school basketball tournament. It was scheduled for the very next week.

Being dedicated to the proposition of drawing no attention to myself in a system where the faculty was often at odds with the administration, I promised I would have an appropriate prayer written and ready to be recorded before the day was out.

At once I regretted my quick compliance with the request, because I realized that by agreeing to it was to make myself complicit in the widespread misunderstanding of the true nature of prayer. Prayer is always to be viewed as a sacred interaction between human beings and God. It is never to be profaned by relegating it to some kind of pro forma performance that intends nothing more than to signal the prelude and/or the beginning of some sports competition or secular meeting.

It should never be recorded nor packaged for public consumption at a secular event as if it were some motto or mantra. And any member of the clergy faced with the invitation to do so should have the good sense to decline. They should instead move forward with determination in the cause of teaching others about the true sacredness of prayer.

When I was a kid growing up in Dallas, my parents often took me and my three brothers to Southwest Conference football games. The events were notorious for pitting two Texas universities, and sometimes the University of Arkansas, against each other in heated battles. The outcomes determined the bragging rights for each team's respective fan base for the coming year. And prior to each Southwest Conference game, by longstanding tradition, some prominent clergyman would offer a prayer.

Even as a child, I wondered about the appropriateness of praying at a football game. And by the time I was an adolescent, I found it humorous that every "Amen" was punctuated with fans yelling at the top of their lungs to give the opposing team hell.

In truth, I bowed my head during these public exhibitions of pseudo-piety, all the while hoping that the preacher at the microphone would hurry through the prayer so that we might get to the long-anticipated kickoff.

One of my favorite stories about prayer concerns a prominent Baptist pastor in Austin, Texas, who in the mid 1950s was invited to offer a prayer at a football game between the Texas Longhorns and some hapless foe. As the story goes, this man approached the microphone and offered a deep and audible sigh before offering the following words: "Almighty God, you know we are not here to pray. Amen."

This sudden and startling break from tradition must have impacted the crowd in any number of ways. It also could have contributed to a new policy of no public invocation before the game.

What I appreciate about this story is multilayered. This pastor taught his corner of the world a great truth: prayer is never to be considered a meaningless, pro forma expression signaling nothing more than the beginning of a secular event. And by reminding his massive audience of the truth, he reclaimed the sacredness of prayer. Perhaps most important of all, he did it by remaining respectful, in that he didn't scold or pontificate or adopt a "holier than thou" attitude. He assumed the role of a humble prophet, long enough to remind people he loved, that prayer is not a spectator sport. It is rather a sacred interaction between people and God, and is therefore to be treated always with reverence.

A second illustration of using prayer to make a prophetic stance is even more powerful.

This story concerns a young Presbyterian pastor who in the 1950s served a large church in Dallas. At the time of his service, the city of Dallas was one of the most segregated cities in the South. For example, following the Supreme Court ruling of 1954 outlawing racial segregation in the nation's public schools, the Dallas Independent School District chose to ignore the ruling altogether, thus continuing the long-held practice of "separate, but equal" schools.

Throughout the years of heated debate about the "rightness" of integration, this young pastor always maintained his position as a champion of integration of the schools and of every other public institution. Needless to say, his stance was not popular with many in his congregation, but the church continued to support him because his sermons were excellent and his love for his people palpable.

The result was an uneasy peace that existed between this young and courageous prophet and his flock.

Everything came to a head the day the Presbytery (the body that oversees all of the Presbyterian churches in North Texas) sent the young pastor a message, asking him to invite all of the Presbyterian youth of North Texas to enjoy an evening of fun, fellowship, dinner, and worship in the church's social hall. If the church hosted such an event, it meant that the congregation's white young people would be sharing a meal and otherwise socializing with the Black youth from the very few Black Presbyterian churches that existed at the time.

Upon reading the Presbytery's request, the pastor must have winced because he knew that such a special evening would be a hard sell to his session, which is the governing body of the church.

At last, the Sunday afternoon arrived when the pastor presented the request to the church elders who composed the session. And just as he expected, the elders balked as they listed all of the reasons why such a proposed event was not at all a good idea.

In truth, there was no debate on the issue, only the old tired, threadbare arguments against race-mixing, the same ones folks in the South had used since prior to the Civil War. When someone called for the vote, that call received an immediate second. Of course, the session voted to reject the Presbytery's request. As far as the elders were concerned, the issue was dead

No doubt, the church elders were both relieved and

satisfied that they had protected their own young people from the culture's determination to force integration upon even their most sacred and private institution. The courts might integrate the public schools, but these good Presbyterians were hell-bent to make certain that integration would not now and could never occur in their church.

With the voting completed, the pastor rose to announce what elders knew to be the obvious conclusion of their meeting. Standing before a group of men, most of whom were old enough to be his father, he said, "The Book of Church Order stipulates that every meeting of the church session should be concluded with a prayer. And, of course, I agree with this practice, but I cannot bring myself to pray over the decision you have made this afternoon, so I will leave you now to pray over yourselves. I'm going home."

Some three hours later, the pastor received a call from a church elder informing him that the session had rescinded their original vote and had instead voted to invite all of the young people of their presbytery (Blacks included) to come to their church to enjoy an evening of fellowship, food, and worship.

The young pastor not only knew the sacredness of prayer and when to pray, but even more he recognized when not to pray.

But I suppose St. Paul was right when he declared to the ages that most of us don't know how to pray.

I was once acquainted with a family where everyone in the family suffered from the truth that the father of four children and the husband to his wife, and self-proclaimed head of the household, was an alcoholic. But this obvious fact was a family secret never to be exposed, lest the father, a fellow named John, resort to a violent revenge on his accusers.

As a result, all four children were afflicted with intense anxiety, while their mother sought medical treatment for her depression. Needless to say, theirs was not a happy home, as they all lived under the constant threat of the father's legendary explosive temper.

Year after painful year, this family somehow managed to muddle through life, all the while becoming more bonded by a shared fear than by any kind of genuine love. And year after year, the father continued to drink and experience brushes with the law, as in vain he attempted to hide from the truth that he was a very sick man in dire need of treatment.

When his beleaguered wife came to me for counsel, I suggested that she seek help from her family physician for her depression and that she pray for her husband. What I could not even imagine was that, in accepting my suggestion, she would weaponize prayer.

Soon after our brief visit, she announced to her family that she would be offering the evening table grace. Her prayer went something like this: "Dear God, we thank you for this good food. Now please help John with his alcoholism, because all of us in this family know he is a miserable drunk."

As expected, the husband erupted in a violent demonstration of rage. He flipped over the family's table before storming out of the house to drive away at speed high enough to get him arrested and incarcerated.

It should be obvious, this is not the way to pray.

And then, there was the ersatz church politician, who in my view, was dedicated to chasing after a little prestige the way a dog chases a rabbit. After being elected to an office that was, at best, meaningless, and a worst, wholly anachronistic, this ambitious little preacher invited his audience to join him in prayer.

Only because I was tired of sitting on a hard church pew for two days, and, therefore close to desperate for some sign of a final benediction to signal the conclusion of this interminable meeting, I glanced at my watch. The hour was straight up one o'clock. I then rose with the congregation to bow my head and to remain silent as several hundred of us from four states listened to this man pray.

Perhaps it was a shot of adrenaline that ignited this man's brain, or the thrill of realizing a dream come true, but whatever it was that fired his system, he launched into a prayer that seemed to cover every subject from death to taxes in a droning monologue that lasted a full seventeen minutes.

I know.

I glanced at my watch again once this exuberant little man showed mercy by uttering his "Amen."

Of course, it is a sin to judge others, nevertheless I walked away from that prayer all but convinced that what I had just endured was a prayer far more intended to impress a man's captured audience than it was to lead us into the sacred experience of talking to God. And forget about listening for any possible—and always subtle—response from Heaven.

As far as I'm concerned, to use prayer as a means to impress anyone is always the wrong way to pray.

The issue of imposing prayers on others, however, arises when they may not be at all interested in praying or in being subjected to an appropriation of God which is not their own. My younger brother, John, served for thirty years as the pastor of the smallest, still active Presbyterian Church in Oklahoma. In addition, he served the community at large as licensed defense attorney and as his small town's municipal judge.

A decade or so before his untimely death in 2008, his community's school board called upon him to advise them concerning the very thorny issue of returning prayer to their public schools. He was quick to remind them that their proposal was against the law, because it violated the 1963 Supreme Court ruling which banned prayer in the nation's public schools.

Following this warning, John rose from his chair for emphasis and announced that he was now ready to remove his lawyer's hat and speak to them as a trained theologian.

"I just have one question," he said, "and it is this: Whose prayer do you propose to pray?"

The school board sat in stunned silence until someone spoke up. "What do you mean, whose prayer?"

"I mean, do you propose to pray a Jewish prayer, or a Buddhist prayer, or a prayer to Sophia, the Goddess of all feminine wisdom, or a Muslim prayer, or a prayer in the name of Jesus Christ?"

Because there was no response to his question, John made a polite exit from the room, only to learn later that evening that the board had voted unanimously to drop the issue of returning prayer to the public schools. John was a wise and good teacher, who recognized that imposing prayer on anyone is always wrong, He knew the words of St. Paul prove that sometimes we just "don't know how to pray."

The very worst way to attempt to pray is to equate partisan politics with genuine piety. Not long ago, a right-wing governor of Texas decided that the country needed him to run for President. As fortune would have it, the country didn't agree. The venue he chose to launch his campaign was a proposed "prayer rally" in a rented Houston football stadium.

The problem here is not that the politician was of any particular party, but rather that by hosting a "prayer rally," this man was more than insinuating that his mandate to run for office was not only blessed by God, but even ordained. And anytime a politician equates his or her political agenda with God's holy will, it is time to question everything about such a position.

Jesus came to Earth to proclaim a new kingdom, but this new order was in no way political. Instead, it was meant to be a kingdom founded on and grounded in love and forever to be marked by grace.

As I read Scripture, I cannot see that Jesus was much interested in politics and/or all that impressed by the politicians of his day. Therefore, I regard it as always wrong to attempt to make our prayers political endorsements for any politician or for any political agenda.

Without question, Jesus was the incarnation of truth,

and that is so, because the ultimate truth is invariably love.

And yet, a Roman politician stood face to face with Jesus and spoke the most absurd question ever uttered by a human being. "What is truth?"

And if today's politicians knew the truth, they would never think it a good idea to organize a prayer rally.

But alas, they will continue to do so, because as St. Paul put it two thousand years ago, "We do not know how to pray."

Chapter 8

"Be still, and know that I am God."

Psalm 46:10

L ife has a way of playing a trick on us. It's not a particularly cruel one, but it is a trick, nevertheless. And it is this: By the circumstances of our birth as totally dependent human beings, we learn from the very earliest days of our lives that we must be the very center of the universe.

All we need do is whimper, and our every need is met. We are fed, and/or our diaper is changed, and we are comfortable again. At least in functional families, this is so.

By the time we reach school age, we have come to the conclusion that this life is pretty much all about us. In general, and in particular, daily life is about getting our emotional and ego needs met.

When we reach adolescence, we have learned to crave attention and seek the approbation of our peers, regardless of the means we employ to accomplish our goal of recognition and popularity. To our ultimate disadvantage, most of us never outgrow this need, and the reason for that is as simple as it is dangerous.

We are blind to our narcissism. We can't and we don't see it, no matter how many people tell us of our self-centeredness.

But Jesus saw it, and understood it for what it is, a wedge separating every self-absorbed human being from becoming one with God. This is why he told Nicodemus he would have to be born again. And this is also why Jesus said, If any want to become my followers, let them deny themselves and take up their cross and follow me. *(Luke 9:23)*

Years ago, I overheard two young businessmen in Dallas discussing their subjective definitions of success. The older of the two offered that if one is not earning at least twice his or her age in annual income, that person is a loser. I've long considered that misguided observation one of the saddest commentaries I've ever encountered.

I never really chased after the "almighty dollar," but as a young, newly-minted seminary graduate, I did make the mistake of allowing myself to become interested in making a name for myself in the old Southern Presbyterian Church. Of course, I had no idea as to how to go about doing that, but I did hope to do something significant enough that others would notice.

And in making this unenlightened commitment, I steeped myself in the great cultural error of believing that this life was about me. By definition, life had to be about my being fulfilled, happy, successful, recognized, appreciated, and even applauded. This error was ingrained in me to such a profound degree that it had become fixed in my unconscious and shackled to the warp and the woof that made up my character.

This belief became a major part of my worldview, and yet, I never saw the need to examine it or to compare my intrinsic belief system to the teachings of Jesus.

This is the great trap most of us stumble into, and when we fall, we remain mired in it until some unexpected and painful occurrence compels us to examine everything about ourselves. If we do that with integrity mixed with uncommon courage, we will come to discover that this gift of our life is not now, nor has it ever been, about us.

No, the truth is that this life is about something much, much greater. The truth is that this life is about us becoming living and breathing expressions—or, if you will, incarnations—of God's love.

The 10th verse of the 46th psalm, which serves as the scriptural heading for this chapter, is a gentle and simple prayer which, if prayed with a pure heart, can shepherd us out of our predilection for self-absorption. The first step is to do as the psalm commands, and become very still.

In doing this, we surrender the need to chase after anything, including money, prestige, and/or success symbols.

Next, by allowing ourselves to confess that God is God, we admit the obvious. We are not God.

Among other things, this means we must relinquish the need to control everything about our lives, including other people.

Living in and with self-absorption is what St. Paul

meant by 'living in the flesh'. The choice is always with us: we can live for ourselves and for our own self-aggrandizement, or we can live in the Spirit, and, thereby enjoy the fruits of the Spirit, one of which is joy.

In my counseling practice over the years, I encountered innumerable folks who were addicted to alcohol or some other drug, and I often wondered why we human beings are so eager to use chemicals we admit will ruin our lives and even destroy us.

As I write these words, our country is experiencing what the experts are calling an opioid epidemic, where hundreds of thousands, if not millions, of people have become addicted to pain killers.

Whenever I encountered an addict seeking help from me, my response was always this: "You're addicted, and I cannot help you until you enter treatment for your addiction. Otherwise, it's like you're asking me to paint your house while it's still on fire. We have to put the fire out with the 12 Steps of Recovery, before we can even think about rebuilding your house and giving it a fresh coat of paint."

Many clients stormed their way out of my office while a few paused to say, "So what do I do?"

My response was automatic and consistent: "Find a 12 Step group, recruit a sponsor, and ask God to restore you to sanity."

Over the years, several of my clients followed my advice and in time, but not overnight, became whole human beings who learned to live in the Spirit. They reaped the rewards of denying themselves and of following Jesus into a whole new way of becoming a new human being.

One of the immeasurable benefits of working the 12 Steps is that it delivers us from a lifetime of self-absorption and takes us to a whole new place where the experience of genuine joy is an everyday occurrence.

And the more I thought about our epidemic of addiction in this country, the more I viewed the problem through the prism of Scripture.

Two thousand years ago St. Paul was so correct and his insight so amazing when he posited that joy is to be discovered in a life lived in the Spirit. It can never to be discovered in one's dedication and devotion to oneself.

But people who live in the flesh, like all of us, long for joy. They choose the simple and easy route to a counterfeit joy through the use of alcohol. Of course, this route leads to nothing greater than misery and suffering, while every deliverance to a new life in the Spirit is to be seen as synonymous with salvation.

Seventeen times in the four Gospels, Jesus says, "Follow me," and after 50 years in the ministry, I now think I know why.

But before we can give any serious consideration to following Jesus, we must first be still and know that God is God.

Chapter 9

The benefits of prayer

The first and foremost benefit of prayer is that it connects us to the Source of the greatest power in the universe, which is love. Love does not originate with us, but rather has its origin in the Spirit we call God.

And the more we connect to that Spirit, the more love can flow through us and into our world.

The simple truth is this: the more one expresses love, the healthier that person will be. In fact, those who do not allow love to flow from them are never happy. How could they be?

For love is the great and eternal truth Jesus came to proclaim through his very incarnation of what St. John described "the Word becoming flesh." Those who get in the way of love flowing from God through them are unwitting strangers to the truth, unhappy folks who are living a lie. They told themselves that someone else, or something other than love, can make them happy.

Perhaps this is why every evening here in the capital city of Texas, as well as throughout the country, local bars and watering holes refer to a brief window of time as "Happy

Hour," when alcohol is a bit cheaper.

The sad truth is that alcohol never made anyone happy. Rather, it has landed countless people in jail, just as it has shattered marriages and wrecked lives in every generation since human kind figured out how to ferment some kind of agricultural product, such as grapes or corn.

If our city council were to pass a "truth in advertising ordinance," every bar or saloon in this city would be required to replace the "Happy Hour" signs with new signage that reads "Drink at your own risk hour," or "Alcohol is addictive and can lead to tragedy hour."

That will never happen, because the "spirits lobby" is far stronger and much wealthier than any organized advocacy on behalf of the Spirit.

So, the best we can hope for is to open the doors of our churches, synagogues, mosques, and other worship centers with the intention of inviting 12-STEP groups to hold regular meetings. We can hope that supporting addicts and alcoholics as they learn how to get out of their own way will further the sacred cause of their becoming the very incarnation of love.

Many years ago, a young woman, a member of the mega-church where I taught, requested that I officiate her father's memorial service. Upon agreeing, I invited her to my office the following day to assist her in planning the service, as well as so I might also learn a bit of salient information regarding her father's life.

Once we were in my office, she spoke of her unconditional love for a man she described as terribly flawed. She described him as an alcoholic, who often abused his wife and children. Between sobs, she recounted a tale of genuine horror regarding her father's arrest and subsequent indictment in a police investigation of the murder of a black man in a small East Texas town.

According to her, a high-dollar, and no doubt slick, lawyer convinced the jury to acquit him. Her father walked out of that court room, free to live out his life as a strident racist and a lifelong supporter of the local Klan.

The more I heard about this man, the more I wished she had not asked me to officiate at his memorial service. Then, my training kicked in and I recalled a request had been made of me as a Minister of the Word and Sacrament in the Presbyterian Church USA. I remembered my responsibility was to offer this man's family a worship experience marked by dignity and grounded in the truth that God's grace is sufficient for us all.

Perhaps the biggest hurdle for me was this young woman's request that she be allowed to play a compact disc of Frank Sinatra's signature ballad, "I Did It My Way," as the prelude to the service. This grieving daughter reported that this one song contained the sum of her deceased father's personal philosophy on how to live his life.

I agreed only because it was way past time, and wholly inappropriate for me to attempt to teach this woman anything. I said nothing and later listened as Frank Sinatra sang a proud paean in praise of narcissism.

I cringed through the entire recorded performance, because what this grieving daughter did not, and probably could not, understand is that according to her own report, her father chose to live his life doing everything his way.

Thus he missed the great blessings inherent in doing life God's way instead.

Once more, St. Paul termed a life lived our way, as a life lived in the "flesh," or what in today's post-Freudian world, what we would more likely call a life lived in the ego. And St. Paul would have us know that a life lived in the "flesh" is a life marked by fornication, impurity, licentiousness, idolatry, enmities, strife, anger, quarrels, dissensions, factions, drunkenness, carousing and the like. *(Galatians 5:19-21)*

Yet what I find so curious about us human beings is that the vast majority choose to do our lives our way. We err in believing that doing life our way is tantamount to living the life of rugged individualism, which for most of us is to be admired and even praised in song and on film.

However, the simple truth is this: doing life our way and on no terms but our own is to live a life as an idolater with the ego serving as the object of our worship and life-long personal devotion. The biggest and thorniest problem with life in the "flesh" is that no real or lasting happiness can ever be derived from such an existence.

I have no idea nor can I present any kind of informed theory as to what is wrong with us as a nation. But even the most casual observer must admit that, as a people, we are terribly divided, to the point that some are predicting, of all things, a second civil war.

Even during my college and seminary years when massive anti-war protests filled our nation's streets, I've never witnessed a people so estranged. At the time I'm writing the closing chapter of this book, a television news anchor has informed me that in the first five months of this year (2022) there have been exactly 198 mass shootings in America.

And in the wake of this tragic number, our political rhetoric has never been so violent.

So, what is the cause?

As to a diagnosis of our collective problem, I'm not nearly smart enough nor sufficiently educated to hazard a guess while employing any high-sounding social scientific term, but I am willing to posit an observation which I hold to be inarguable: We as a people, and, of course as individuals, have not only lost our way, we have also lost our very grounding.

Our grounding is in the Spirit.

We have come to rely so much on ourselves and even place our trust in our own intellect that we have both consciously and unconsciously separated ourselves from God. And what I find so fascinating about all of this is that even our churches—our once hallowed institutions—have joined the fray by identifying with the cultural divide.

Today the religious right has morphed into a strong base for right-wing politicians, while the more moderate and/or liberal churches function in much the same way for left-of-center candidates. When I was a kid, churches could be counted on to stay clear of politics, but today's churches too often view themselves as quasi-political action committees, devoted to seeing their chosen—and some would even claim, God-ordained—candidate get elected.

I'm even familiar with churches where folks are told to vote for a particular candidate or forfeit the right to call themselves a Christian. Throughout the whole of my career, I always encouraged the folks in the pews to vote, but I never told them how they should vote.

As a people and as individuals, we stand in need of healing like never before. Most simply put, we stand in prodigious need of the "fruit of the Spirit," as St. Paul so elegantly described the gifts of love, joy, peace, patience, kindness, generosity, faithfulness, gentleness, and self-control.

These amazing gifts are given to those who choose to pray with such heartfelt sincerity and frequency. They will then live in a whole new way or in the way St. Paul described as "life in the Spirit."

Since my retirement following a stroke some ten years ago, I have chosen to live a life where I have separated myself on purpose from groups of folks and crowds. As a result, I speak to very few people on a daily basis, and never do I find myself in the role of being subjected to the kinds of interesting questions posed to me on a regular basis for more than four decades.

But, if some unhappy soul were to ask me how he or she could be happy, I would answer that question in one simple, revolutionary word.

"Pray."

And then, I would leave the rest to God.

ABOUT THE AUTHOR

Bob Lively was born and raised in Dallas, Texas, where he was educated in the Dallas public schools. He is a graduate of Austin College and of Austin Presbyterian Theological Seminary, and both schools have named him a distinguished alumnus. He was ordained in 1973 by the old Southern Presbyterian Church, which is now the Presbyterian Church USA. He served pastorates in Arkansas and in Texas. For the past half century, he served the church as a pastor, community activist, newspaper columnist, certified pastoral counselor, college instructor, seminary lecturer, teacher, retreat leader, campus minister and recovery center chaplain.

He is married to Dr. Mary Lynn Rice-Lively, a retired associate dean at the University of Texas. He is the author of 15 books, with this one being his last. He is an award-winning short story writer and for 23 years he wrote a column in *The Austin*

portrait by Gregory T. Smith

American-Statesman.

He is a founding minister of the Stewpot ministry, which at last count had served over eight million meals to the homeless of Dallas. Bob is also the founding minister of the Community Ministry of the First Presbyterian Church of Dallas.

He is the father to one daughter, Sarah Hill, and a grandfather to Henry Hill.

He is honorably retired, and he and his wife live on an acre in the hills west of Austin.

Made in the USA
Columbia, SC
20 September 2022